A GOOD BOOK PRACTICAL GUIDE

PLANTING
A BIBLE
GARDEN

Text Crown copyright © 1987,
revised © 1997
This edition copyright
© 1997Angus Hudson Ltd/
Tim Dowley & Peter Wyart trading as
Three's Company

Published in the USA
by Fleming H. Revell, a division of
Baker Book House Company
P.O. Box 6287, Grand Rapids, MI
49516-6287

Library of Congress Cataloging-in-
Publication Data
Hepper, F.N.
    Planting a Bible garden/F. Nigel Hepper.
       p. cm.
    Includes bibliographical references and
indexes.
    ISBN 0-8007-1756-2 (hardcover)
    1. Plants in the Bible. 2. Gardening. I.
Title.
SB454.3.B52H47 1998
635—dc21
                                       97-39355

Designed by Peter Wyart,
Three's Company

Worldwide coedition organized and
produced by Angus Hudson Ltd,
Concorde House,
Grenville Place, Mill Hill,
London NW7 3SA, England
Tel: +44 181 959 3668
Fax: +44 181 959 3678

Printed in Singapore

Acknowledgments

I am grateful for helpful comments on
the draft of the text by my colleague
Brian Mathew of Kew Herbarium,
also Geoffrey Collins, formerly at
Hampton Court Gardens, and Samuel
Sprunger of Basel for a Central
European viewpoint, both of whom
were trained at the School of
Horticulture, Royal Botanic Gardens,
Kew.
    Quotations from the Bible are
mainly from the New Revised
Standard Version.
    The Egyptian vignette is from
Wilkinson's *Manners and Customs*.

*The LORD God took the man and put him
in the garden of Eden to till it and keep it.*
Genesis 2:15

*To everyone who conquers, I will give
permission to eat from the tree of life that is
in the paradise of God.*
Revelation 2:7

Cover and opposite: Part of the author's
Bible garden.
All photographs are by the author,
except pl. 98, which is by S. Holmes.

PLANTING

A BIBLE

GARDEN

F. NIGEL HEPPER

A practical reference guide for the home gardener, schools, colleges and churches in all climates of the world

Drawings and photographs by the author

Fleming H. Revell

A Division of Baker Book House Co
Grand Rapids, Michigan 49516

Foreword

The Bible is a collection of books whose composition spans many centuries. Not only does it record the events and beliefs important to the people of its time, but it also chronicles the development of a moral and religious system whose influence continues to the present.

The accounts found in the Bible are told within the context of human existence. Plants and their products are such an integral part of people's lives, that it is not surprising that they have been incorporated into these narratives. It may come as a surprise, though, to discover how often one encounters plants in the scriptures. The range of such references is wide, from descriptions of their everyday uses to their mention in parables and teachings.

Regardless of a person's religious convictions, it is clear that the Bible has held, and will continue to hold, great significance to people. To many, its verses offer counsel and inspiration. In other cases, it is a book of historical or literary value. One way to draw closer to this book and learn more about it is to create a table link to the writings. Undoubtedly this is why Bible gardens hold such appeal.

A number of botanical gardens and other institutions in many places have developed formal displays of plants native to the Middle East. For example, the Biblical Garden in the Shoenberg Temperate House at the Missouri Botanical Gardens has been a popular feature with our visitors.

For many, seeing plants tied to the writings in this ancient text can be a thought-provoking experience. Visiting a display garden is one way to learn more about these plants. Another more direct way to study them would be to plan your own Bible garden. It is always a challenge to design a garden and choose appropriate plants, and perhaps this is even more the case with gardens built around a theme. Luckily, Nigel Hepper's book offers a blueprint for such an endeavour. Based on biblical research, many suggestions are given for choosing probable candidate plants, even with suggested alternatives when 'true' Bible plants are not available. By making these suggestions in relation to specific verses of the Bible, the choice of plants to grow can have very deep personal meaning.

For botanists and horticulturists, this book has another dimension. By including descriptions of many species, Hepper highlights the rich botanical diversity of this part of the world. The choices for the gardener are thus many. Hints on cultivation can help the serious gardener understand how best to develop and maintain his or her garden space.

In the final analysis, this book is an indispensable reference for the serious gardener who plans to make the pages of the Bible come alive.

Peter H. Raven
Director, Missouri Botanical Garden,
St Louis, Missouri

Pl. 6a. Massed poppies *Papaver rhoeas* in an olive grove in Crete.

Contents

Introduction

The idea of taking a theme for a garden is new to many gardeners, yet it is as old as the oldest herb garden. There are also water gardens, heath gardens, wild gardens and even gardens composed of trees (arboreta), so why not Bible gardens? Here is a splendid theme for a school, college or church-yard, as well as for your own private garden, using plants mentioned in the Bible. It is a novel way of bringing the Bible to life, showing the living Creation; the Old Testament pictures God the life-giver, the New Testament shows new life in Christ.

If you read the Bible with an eye on the references to plants, fruits, food, timber, gardens and agriculture, you will be astonished how frequently they are mentioned. There is hardly a chapter without such a reference and in many chapters there are several. Look at the very first chapter of Genesis: 'Then God said, "Let the earth put forth vegetation: plants yielding seed, and fruit trees of every kind on earth that bear fruit with the seed in it"' (1:11). In the second chapter we read that 'The LORD God planted a garden in Eden, in the east; and there he put the man whom he had formed. Out of the ground the LORD God made to grow every tree that is pleasant to the sight and good for food, the tree of life also in the midst of the garden, and the tree of the knowledge of good and evil' (2:8-9). In Genesis 3 the ground is cursed because of the sin of Adam and Eve: 'Thorns and thistles it shall bring forth for you; and you shall eat the plants of the field' (3:18); in chapter 4 there is Cain, 'a tiller of the ground', who murdered his sheep-keeping brother Abel; and so it continues. By the time of the Exodus from Egypt, Moses was laying down the code for good husbandry of the land, which is recorded in the book of Leviticus (Chapters 25 and 26). And the Lord promised his people a good land 'of wheat and barley, of vines and fig

trees and pomegranates, a land of olive trees and honey' (Deuteronomy 8:8).

The Psalms frequently refer to vegetation in one form or another. Thus the very first Psalm likens good people to 'trees planted by streams of water, which yield their fruit in its season, and their leaves do not wither' . . . but the wicked 'are like chaff that the wind drives away'. Some of the references are general, while others are to particular plant species such as the cedar of Lebanon (Psalm 104:16). The Song of Solomon is a rich source of plant references: vines and pomegranates, mandrakes and lilies, and spices and myrrh. Some of them were well-known wild flowers and cultivated plants, while others were exotic imports.

Clearly, there is great scope for a garden using these plants since they range from small herbs to huge trees, and their habitats from marshes to tropical deserts. The possibilities are so wide that only the great botanical gardens of the world, such as Kew and Missouri, or Neot Kedumim in Israel, can hope to represent all or most of them. You will have to select those that may be grown in your region given your facilities. It is useless to attempt to grow tropical plants in, say, England without a greenhouse, and conversely temperate plants may succumb in the tropics. On the other hand, a resourceful gardener can use every skill at his disposal to overcome such limitations.

Gardens in the Bible

In biblical times gardens were essentially for fruit trees, herbs and vegetables, rather than to display the beauty of flowers, as are many gardens today. Most scholars now believe that the word 'Eden', used as the name of the place where God 'planted a garden' (Genesis 2:8; 3:23), has come to us from a Sumerian or Akkadian word meaning 'plain'. That is, the

garden was situated on a plain and Eden is not a proper name at all. Subsequently it became known as 'Paradise' which is an anglicised form of the Persian word for a walled garden. Such a walled garden would belong to a wealthy man and in dry regions it needed a ready supply of water for irrigation. King Solomon's had pools and he boasted: 'I made great works; I built houses and planted vineyards for myself; I made myself gardens and parks, and planted in them all kinds of fruit trees. I made myself pools from which to water the forest of growing trees' (Ecclesiastes 2:4-6). The King's garden in Jerusalem was also near a water source, the Pool of Siloam (Jeremiah 52:7). In well-watered Jezreel the wicked Ahab wanted to convert Naboth's vineyard into a vegetable garden or a 'garden of herbs' because it was near his palace (1 Kings 21). Vegetables and fragrant herbs were highly prized in ancient times, as nowadays.

Elsewhere in the biblical lands Ashurnasirpal, king of Assyria, trained gardeners to maintain botanical and zoological gardens and a park; and the hanging gardens of Babylon were one of the Seven Wonders of the ancient world. In Egypt there were ornamental gardens such as the one drawn on the wall of a tomb belonging to a general in the army of Pharaoh Amenophis III, about 1400 B.C. The garden was walled and the geometrical layout allowed the numerous criss-crossing irrigation channels to reach the vines trained over pergolas, as well as the date palms and other fruit trees such as pomegranates. The rectangular ponds in Ancient Egyptian gardens were gay with water-lilies, especially the blue-flowered ones which were favoured for their scent. Later on, the Greeks enjoyed gardens, and the Romans, too, had delightful ones, such as may be seen reconstructed in the courtyards at Pompeii dating from the New Testament period. Archaeologists have been able to trace the fine roots of trees and locate the positions of the trees themselves.

The trees planted in ancient gardens were usually fruit trees such as olive, fig and pomegranate. These little orchards were shady retreats like the garden of Gethsemane – the name literally means 'of the oil press' – on the Mount of Olives, where it was Jesus' custom to go (Luke 22:39). The rock-hewn sepulchre in which Jesus' body was laid must have been set in a garden since after his resurrection, when he revealed himself to Mary Magdalene, she supposed him to be the gardener (John 20:15-16).

In this book when I refer to biblical gardens I do not necessarily mean the kind mentioned above, but gardens of any design which include the various plants mentioned in the Bible; and first we need to know what plants these are.

Pl. 1. A Bible garden created by the author at Redcliffe College, then in London.

The study of plants mentioned in the Bible

The study of biblical plants has been going on for centuries, principally because translators of the Hebrew and Greek scriptures needed to know how to render the names in their own languages. This was often very difficult as the plants (and animals) of the biblical lands were imperfectly known to scientists, never mind to linguists. During the eighteenth and nineteenth centuries several expeditions from Europe were sent to the Middle East in order to find out what living creatures and plants occur there. Even today scientists are still discovering new species and finding out more about the life-histories of those already known.

All this biological study has been coupled with linguistic scholarship to identify names in one language and translate them into another. Of course the writers of the Bible were not botanists themselves and used words that were imprecise or stood for whole groups of plants, such as 'tree' or 'thorns'. Sometimes scholars can distinguish those words that indicate, say, a particular kind of thorny plant, and speculate which of several it might be. So when it comes to the different translations of the Bible, there is considerable variation.

When the scholars were working on the King James Bible (that is, the Authorised Version), published in 1611, they sometimes translated a Greek word by using the English name of a suitable plant that fitted the context. For example, in the Parable

of the Tares, as it has become known, the weeds said to have been mixed with the good wheat seeds were called in Greek *zizania*; this is the darnel grass, which bears poisonous grain, but the translators of the King James Version could not have known that and inserted the word 'tares', a noxious leguminous weed of English cornfields at that time. Similarly, the acacia tree was unknown in seventeenth-century England, and the scholars did not translate its Hebrew name at all, but left it as *shittim*. These are examples that have been resolved, but there are others that are still a matter of opinion and discussion. Take, for instance, the coniferous trees. Although there is little dispute about the cedar of Lebanon, there is no agreement on which Hebrew words should be applied to the pine, cypress, fir and juniper. Consequently there are different names in the many versions of the Bible.

This has presented me with a problem as to which species to recommend in this book.* I admit that in some cases there is a compromise with several species being mentioned, while for others I have firmly assigned the species that I consider to be correct or appropriate for the context. Sometimes I have interpreted this widely in order to provide a good selection of plants for Bible gardens. Thus it would be a pity to limit yourself to only one 'flower of the field' when there are many beautiful plants in the

Holy Land that are suitable for a Bible garden. So I have proposed, in this case, anemone, poppy, crown daisy, and others.

While many plants referred to in the Bible are readily available from commercial sources, a few are difficult or impossible to obtain. I have tried to list alternative species in most cases to help to overcome this problem. There is another advantage in mentioning alternatives even if the proper species is available; namely, it enables you to select a plant that you know should be successful in your region, in preference to another that may not do as well. So if you know that a certain species will not survive the winter in your area, select a similar hardier one of the same genus. There are usually more alternatives than the ones I have listed, but space forbids a long catalogue.

Should you wish to choose other species not mentioned here, there are many horticultural and botanical dictionaries and encyclopedias available in public libraries that supply such information. However, you do need to be cautious in order to select sensible alternatives. I would not advocate growing a substitute plant whose growth form is wildly different from the original, even though both belong to the same genus.

*Research for my accounts of biblical plants in *The Illustrated Bible Dictionary* (1980), *The Book of Bible Knowledge* (1982), *Bible Plants at Kew* (1985) and *Illustrated Encyclopedia of Bible Plants* (1992) form the basis of my selection.

Planning your Bible Garden

Happily there are no hard and fast rules to follow – in fact there are really no rules at all related to planning a Bible garden. You can make it as you wish, projecting your own interests, enthusiasms and personality. Of course, there are horticultural and botanical aspects to consider as well as design practice, but this is normal with any garden. A special-theme garden deserves special attention from the outset.

The simplest way is to adapt your existing garden by inter-planting it with biblical species and labelling them accordingly. This is what I do in my own garden at home. I have several small patches here and there devoted to particular species, as it is inappropriate, for instance, to have onions and other vegetables in the herbaceous border. I also separate the cereals and inter-sow them with thistles and poppies to form an attractive mini-cornfield. If you have room for trees and shrubs, plant as many of the biblical species as you can, as they help to give all-the-year interest when herbaceous plants are over. Greenhouse plants and tender species can be incorporated during the summer, so make sure that your design accounts for them.

If you have sufficient space at school, college or church to devote an area specifically to a Bible garden, the initial design will be an important factor in its success. For example, you may wish to have separate displays of vegetables, fruits, spices and herbs, and so on, or to adopt an ecological theme with aquatic, desert, woodland and field plants. Perhaps you can think of other groupings that would enhance the display. Whatever the design, be sure to keep the scale appropriate with small beds and narrow paths so that visitors can see the plants and read the labels. Public gardens need to provide access for bigger groups of people and to spread out the displays with larger clumps instead of individual plants. The needs of disabled and handicapped visitors must be kept in mind. Can you, for instance, use a sloping path in place of a flight of steps? Carefully positioned seats transform a garden into a place of tranquillity, prayer and meditation.

The choice of site is vital: a shady damp place is sure to be a disappointment, whereas an open well-drained site with light soil is best for these Mediterranean plants. See whether you can make a level site more interesting by creating undulations or adapting a bank to give a rock-garden. Even the excavations from a pool can be used to good purpose. If you want to make a pool your centrepiece, it should be in a sunny place and not over-shadowed by trees. It is as well to look ahead when planting trees and make sure they will not cast their shade over the garden as a whole. An important part of your planning should be how to maintain it after construction – the work of knowledgeable weeding, sowing, propagation and other jobs should not be left to unskilled labourers. These are just a few ideas which may be supplemented by books on garden design and by visiting other gardens, especially Bible gardens already in existence (p. 93).

Labelling the plants in your Bible garden

Good labelling can transform a miscellaneous, obscure collection of plants into an interesting and instructive garden. You will probably want to adapt the labelling according to your own particular requirement, either for a private garden, or for one attached to a college or church where the labels will be read by many visitors, but the principles of clarity and information apply to both.

Very large labels are likely to be too obtrusive, and I would advise choosing ones that can be read clearly, yet do not dominate the display. Plastic labels may be ordered from the suppliers listed on page 93, or sometimes may be purchased at garden centres. Anodised aluminium tickets are difficult to read as the wording has to be written in pencil along their length, and as they hang down they must be read sideways. I suggest square plastic labels set in the ground or hanging on tree trunks, with bold lettering that can be read by adults standing upright as it is tiresome to have to bend down to scrutinise every label! Engraved laminated plastic labels are even better if you can afford them. For the garden I designed at St George's College, Jerusalem, special pottery labels were made, like those used for the college rooms inside. They are glued to short metal stands.

Restrict the information to such items as the common name in your language, the scientific name (even the Hebrew or Greek for the erudite!) and a Bible reference. It may be possible to quote a verse or to summarise a reference, for example:

Darnel grass, *Lolium temulentum*
Parable of the Tares, Matthew 13

As to the means of lettering your labels, I find it difficult to be sure that so-called 'permanent' black inks do not wash away in the rain. Chinagraph is perhaps the best crayon. A very satisfactory alternative to hand-lettering is Dymo self-adhesive tape stamped with the wording and carefully cut to fit the plastic label. Most of mine have survived the vagaries of English weather for several years. Be sure that the labels are new ones or at least that they are thoroughly washed before sticking on the wording.

If visitors have to guide themselves around the garden, I suggest an introductory plan and explanation on a board near the entrance. Alternatively, a printed or duplicated leaflet could provide additional information which gives wide scope for teaching aspects coupled with, say, Bible study groups. In situations where the garden may be threatened by vandalism, such leaflets could take the place of vulnerable labels, with the plants marked by numbers corresponding to the notes and plan.

Sketch plan of a Bible Garden

A. Cereals e.g. wheat, barley, tares, grasses

B. Flowers e.g. anemone, narcissus, tulip, star-of-Bethlehem, crown daisy, thistles

C. Vegetables e.g. beans, onions, leeks, garlic, cucumber

D. Spices and Herbs e.g. coriander, dill, mint, chicory, wormwood

E. Pool e.g. waterlily, reeds, reed-mace

F. Seat

G. Arch with vine

1. Almond
2. Apple (espalier)
3. Passion flower
4. Myrtle
5. Viburnum
6. Fig (overhanging)
7. Judas tree
8. Broom
9. Liquidambar
10. Bay
11. Cypress
12. Box
13. Crown-of-thorns
14. Roses
15. Rue, Sage
16. Rock-roses

The naming of plants

Some plants have well-known and accurate common English names, but many more have not. A book of this kind frequently mentions obscure plants that may only be known to botanists. Plants of economic importance, such as flax which yields linen and linseed oil, are unambiguous, but even the fig presents a problem in so far as there are two kinds of fig in the Middle East, as well as many others elsewhere. Instead, therefore, of speaking simply of 'the fig', it is necessary to qualify it, differentiating the *common* fig from the *sycomore* fig.

The numerous species of wild plants of no particular economic importance growing in the Bible lands usually have no English names. Local people may know them by their vernacular names in Hebrew or Arabic, but such are of little value to English readers. For this reason it is much more satisfactory to use the botanical name. Some people are discouraged by these Latin names and unwilling to master them, but they are (or should be) both unambiguous and internationally understood.

The full name has two parts: the generic name and specific epithet. For example, the well-known poppy anemone, familiar in florists' shops and gardens, is scientifically called *Anemone coronaria*. The category genus, in this case *Anemone*, is used for a broad range of similar plants or species, each of which has its own specific epithet: thus *Anemone coronaria* (abbreviated to *A. coronaria*). Similarly, the myrtle is *Myrtus communis*, and the oleander is *Nerium oleander*. With the anemone, it so happens that the English plant name and the scientific generic name are the same, but this is not usually the case.

One further category needs to be mentioned. The anemone belongs to the buttercup family or the *Ranunculaceae* (after *Ranunculus*, the buttercup). The family is a larger assemblage of more or less similar or related plants, and it is often convenient to be able to place an unfamiliar plant in its family. The family name in Latin can usually be recognised by its suffix, *-aceae*. Once the family of an unfamiliar plant is known, it is possible to recognise family characteristics and perhaps to compare with greater

ease and accuracy those that differ. In the plant index at the end of this book the family is given for each genus.

A few more examples may help to explain the terms. The sycomore fig, *Ficus sycomorus*, is in the mulberry family, *Moraceae*; barley, *Hordeum vulgare*, is in the grass family, *Gramineae* (or *Poaceae*); the cedar of Lebanon, *Cedrus libani*, is in the pine family, *Pinaceae*.

Strictly speaking, the name of the botanist who coined the Latin name should be added, usually in abbreviated form, for example the name of the famous eighteenth-century Swedish botanist Linnaeus frequently appears simply as L., as in *Anemone coronaria* L. When a species originally described in one genus is later transferred to another, the name of the first authority is retained alongside the successor: thus Linnaeus named a species of thistle as *Carduus syriacus*; this was later transferred by Cassini to the genus *Notobasis*, and the full citation is therefore *Notobasis syriaca* (L.) Cass. For the sake of completeness I have given these authors of botanical names in the index.

Pl. 2. Part of the Bible Garden at Saint George's College, Jerusalem, with a vine arch, a fig tree and pomegranate bushes behind.

Plants to Grow in your Bible Garden

The following species-by-species section has been arranged according to the life-form or habitat of the plants concerned. The chosen groupings are:

1. **Annuals**
2. **Perennials**
3. **Shrubs and small trees**
4. **Large trees**
5. **Water plants**
6. **Tender plants**

Within each chapter the order is alphabetical by genus, each generic name being coupled with the plant's English name. Used together with the index, this will enable you to plan your garden and to look up each plant reference easily.

At the beginning of each entry there is usually a note indicating where the plant is mentioned in the Bible and giving some idea of the context. A brief description of the plant is supplemented by an illustration (fig.) and sometimes by a colour photograph (pl.). Notes on the cultivation of each species are provided in terms that should apply anywhere in the world. Hence there are references to 'early spring' and 'midsummer' instead of to months of the year which would apply, say, in England but not in Australia. Warm and tropical countries are also catered for, widening the scope yet further.

Finally, each entry provides the Latin name of the biblical species with notes on its distribution, flowering time and so on. Often one or two alternative species are listed in case the true one is unobtainable or will not grow in your area.

Pl. 3. Poppy anemone *Anemone coronaria*.

Pl. 4. Crown daisy *Chrysanthemum coronarium*.

Pl. 5. Hollyhock *Alcea setosa*.

Palestine

0 10 20 Mi
0 10 20 30 Km

• Dan

• Acre

Sea of
Galilee

•Haifa

Tiberias •

• Nazareth

• Caesarea

MEDITERRANEAN SEA

River Jordan

• Nablus

• Tel Aviv

• Amman

• Jericho

• Jerusalem
• Bethlehem

• Ashkelon

En-Gedi •

Dead
Sea

• Beer-sheba

1
Annuals

Although the word 'annual' strictly applies to those plants that complete their life span within a year, it is often used for many other garden plants that are longer lived but are treated as if they were annuals. Onions, for example, are biennials (with a life span of two years) but they are harvested after the first season, to be used as vegetables. Most of the biblical species grouped as 'annuals' are in fact short-lived but they are an important element of any Bible garden. On the other hand, annuals present a problem: you may have an unattractive gap in the garden after they have matured or flowered. It is often better to sow annuals in small patches between permanent low shrubs than to devote larger areas which will later be dull expanses of soil. Successional sowings are another way of ensuring a continuous representation.

In temperate countries three types of annuals are recognised: hardy, half hardy and tender. These all require different treatment. Tropical climates where the temperature is not a governing factor sometimes have the dry season as the limiting period for the cultivation of annuals.

In your garden choose a site that is open to as much sunlight as possible. Dig it deeply and incorporate compost or manure – many of the annuals are 'weeds' naturally occurring in waste places where decaying vegetation has enriched the soil. The soil needs to be well-drained but moisture retentive, otherwise annuals with

Pl. 7. Black mustard *Brassica nigra*.

shallow roots quickly dry out and the whole plant is either dwarfed or withers up completely.

Sowing
Hardy annuals can be sown outside in spring where they are to flower or mature. In milder climates they may do better when sown the previous autumn. This, in fact, is the prevailing growth pattern in the Mediterra-nean area where the autumn rains cause germination, and slow growth continues during the cool period. With the onset

of spring and the raising of the day and night temperatures, growth increases and before the moisture dries up the annuals burst forth into a blaze of colourful flowering.

Scatter your flower seeds but sow your vegetables in lines to give a neat bed. Sow sparingly so as not to crowd the seedlings. Even so, you will need to thin out when the seedlings are recognisable – just pull them up between finger and thumb, leaving enough to form a display. In practice you may

have to thin out several times to avoid overcrowding. You can, of course, try repositioning some of them. Most seedlings transplant satisfactorily if they are carefully lifted, firmly planted and well watered in. Flowering annuals, such as the crown daisy, continue for many weeks, providing they do not dry at the roots and a continual supply of new flowers is encouraged by cutting off the old ones at regular intervals – such cutting is impractical with the thistles! Several of the annuals are grown for the sake of their fruit and seeds – the spicy dill and coriander, the cereal grains of barley and wheat, and the broad beans – so harvest them at the best time, as indicated in the notes under each species.

Half hardy annuals require to be raised in warm conditions, and then planted outside. Cucumbers usually need this treatment as they are tropical plants. They are killed by frost so must not be planted out until all danger is past and the ground has heated a little.

Sub-tropical annuals, such as the water melon, require high temperatures throughout the growing season.

A point to remember about annuals is that they grow quickly and may need the support of sticks or string to prevent their falling over. Supply support in good time or it may be too late since it is difficult to correct a fallen plant. Finally, keep them free of weeds by hoeing or hand-weeding.

Leeks, Onions and Garlic (*Allium*)

These can be taken together not only because they belong to the same genus but as they are all mentioned in the same scriptural verse: 'We remember the fish we used to eat in Egypt for nothing, the cucumbers, the melons, the leeks, the onions, and the garlic; but now our strength is dried up, and there is nothing at all but this manna to look at' (Numbers 11:5-6) – thus the Israelites complained as they followed Moses through the Wilderness, seeking the Promised Land.

Leeks are long and narrow without the bulbous base typical of onions and garlic. Onions have their bulbs composed of concentric fleshy leaf bases, while the garlic bulb has separate scales commonly called 'cloves'. They all produce a round head of mauve or whitish flowers on a tall stem in the second year if they are left.

Pl. 8. Leek *Allium porrum*.

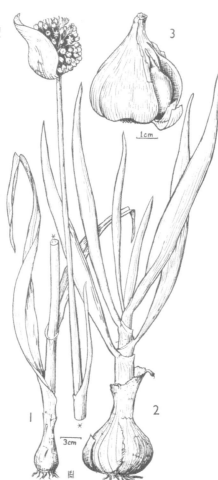

Fig. 1/1. Leek *Allium porrum* plant; 1/2. Onion *A. cepa* plant; 1/3. Garlic *A. sativum* bulb.

Cultivation

Leeks: sow the seeds during the winter or early spring in a seedbed, transplanting the seedlings 15cm (6in.) apart in early summer into rich soil. They will be ready for cooking the following autumn and winter

Onions: either sow seeds or plant sets (tiny bulbs) in early spring. If seedlings are raised, they will need to be either transplanted or thinned out to 15cm (6in.) apart. The bed should be firm and of rich soil. When the bulbs have developed after six months, dry them off before storing.

Garlic: pull apart a bulb and plant the cloves 15cm (6in.) apart in light rich soil in early spring. Lift and store in summer when the bulbs have formed.

Species

Allium cepa, onion, W. Asia, flowering stems are hollow, about 1m (3ft) high, flowers dark mauve; many varieties with large bulbs, leaves hollow (see fig. 1/2)

A. porrum, leek, probably originated in W. Asia, flowering stems over 1m (3ft) high, flowers pale mauve, leaves flat (see fig. 1/1 and pl. 8)

A. sativum, garlic, origin obscure, flowering stems about 80cm (32in.) high, flowers whitish not setting seed, leaves flat (see fig. 1/3)

Dill (*Anethum*)

Several herbs were mentioned by Jesus as being tithed by the scribes and Pharisees who neglected more important matters: 'Woe to you, scribes and Pharisees, hypocrites! For you tithe mint, dill, and cummin, and have neglected the weightier matters of the law: justice and mercy and faith' (Matthew 23:23). One of these plants, the dill (not the 'anise' of earlier biblical translations) is an annual member of the parsley family (*Umbelliferae* or *Apiaceae*) and has similarities with that well-known herb. Dill, like parsley, has a long taproot and the stem grows to 1m (3ft) or more in height, topped by a flat head of greenish yellow flowers in summer. The dissected foliage is light and decorative and may be used fresh to flavour pickled cucumbers. It is the small seeds, however, that are important for their spicy flavour. They are aromatic and used, like the more familiar caraway seeds, in cookery and pickles. Medicinally dill-water is sometimes used as a carminative.

Cultivation

Like all spicy herbs dill needs plenty of light and air in open moist well-drained ground. Sow the seeds sparingly in early spring, thinning the plants 20cm (8in.) apart to allow enough room for them to develop. Do not

Pl. 9. Dill *Anethum graveolens*.

Species

Anthemis chia, Mediterranean, annual, 10-20cm (4-8in.) high, seeds would probably need to be gathered from wild plants as they are not usually on sale

A. nobilis (or *Chamaemelum nobile*), common chamomile, Europe, perennial, 30cm (12in.) high, seeds obtainable commercially

Matricaria recutita (or *M. chamomilla*), wild chamomile, Europe, annual, 30cm (12in.) high, seeds may be offered in wild-flower packets or gathered wild

Calendula arvensis, marigold, Mediterranean, is another attractive species with smaller flowers than the blowzy *C. officinalis*, the pot marigold, from S. Europe

transplant or the taproot may be damaged. Remember that the flowering stem is quite tall and it will be full grown by late summer when the seeds should be collected before they fall naturally.

Fig. 2. Dill *Anethum graveolens*.

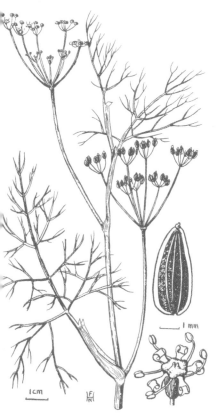

Species

Anethum graveolens S. Europe and W. Asia (see fig. 2 and pl. 9)

Chamomile (*Anthemis, Matricaria*)

One of the biblical 'flowers of the field', related to the crown daisy (see p. 16); there are many species, all with similar daisy-like flowers with yellow centres fringed by white ligules. Some are annuals with a rather erect, bushy growth; others are perennials, tending to spread laterally. They can become troublesome if allowed to seed freely; common chamomile is perennial and a prostrate form can be planted as a lawn with fragrant leaves that may be used for chamomile tea.

Cultivation

As Crown Daisy (p. 16)

Mustard (*Brassica*)

It is a puzzle why the mustard seed was chosen for the parable when Jesus said: 'With what can we compare the kingdom of God, or what parable will we use for it? It is like a mustard seed, which, when sown upon the ground, is the smallest of all the seeds on earth; yet when it is sown it grows up and becomes the greatest of all shrubs, and puts forth large branches, so that the birds of the air can make nests in its shade' (Mark 4:30-32 also Luke 17:6). Traditionally, following the Greek word *sinapi*, this is the black mustard (*Brassica nigra*) which is a tall annual *herb* with small, but not minute, seeds. It is a close relative of the cabbage and produces lobed leaves around its base and a mass of yellow, four-petalled flowers. The narrow fruit pods are held erect and close to the stem. The yellow table mustard is prepared commercially from its hot, oily seeds.

Cultivation

Sow seeds, like other members of the cabbage family, in early spring, thinning or planting out to about 30cm (12in.). An open site with good garden soil enriched with manure is advisable. The masses of bright yellow flowers are very decorative in early summer and the pods can be left to ripen in midsummer, when a lesser flowering may occur.

Species

Brassica nigra, black mustard, Europe and Asia, often sold as 'mustard and cress' for salads in the young seedling stage; mustard seeds are also obtainable separately from cress: 1-1.5m (3-5ft) (see fig. 3 and pl. 7)

Sinapis alba, white mustard, Europe and Near East, cultivated as green manure and for its seeds for the manufacture of table mustard; a smaller plant than black mustard but an appropriate substitute

Fig. 3. Black mustard *Brassica nigra*.

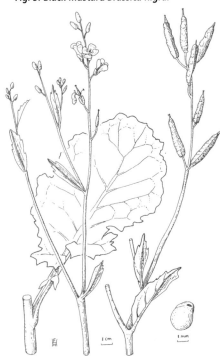

Pl. 10. Corn marigold (*Chrysanthemum segetum*) on waste ground in springtime.

Crown Daisy, Corn Marigold (*Chrysanthemum*)

Many roadsides, field margins and waste places in the Holy Land are wreathed with these beautiful flowers – some of the spectacular weeds or wild flowers characteristic of the Mediterranean spring and a good addition to any biblical garden. Perhaps they are the 'flowers of the field' or 'grass' mentioned in a number of scriptures (Isaiah 40:6; James 1:10; 1 Peter 1:24-25) since they quickly flower and fade, just as human life passes away.

A member of the daisy family (*Compositae*), the crown daisy is an erect annual 50-80cm (20-31in.) high, with finely divided leaves. It grows quickly and, providing it does not dry up, produces large yellow flowers over much of the summer when it is a useful cut flower for small vases.

See also Chamomile (page 15).

Cultivation

Sow seeds either inside in deep boxes or preferably outside in late spring (or autumn in mild areas) where they are to flower.

Transplant or thin out to 10cm (4in.) apart, keeping the soil moist until they are established. An open, sunny, situation is essential, preferably on light soil. Cut off dead flowers to ensure a succession, but leave a few to ripen seeds if required.

Species

Chrysanthemum coronarium, crown daisy, Mediterranean region, flowers typically all yellow but var. *discolor* with banded cream flowers often occurs among them; cultivated varieties available through seed merchants exhibit a wide range of colours including pinks and banded flowers (see fig. 4 and pl. 4)

C. segetum, corn marigold, a similar daisy common in Europe and the Mediterranean region, only 20-40cm (8-16in.) high, with waxy leaves and bright yellow flowers (see pl. 10)

Fig. 4. Crown daisy *Chrysanthemum coronarium*.

Pl. 11. Coriander *Coriandrum sativum*.

Coriander (*Coriandrum*) and Cumin (*Cuminum*)

Both these annual plants belong to the parsley family, *Umbelliferae* or *Apiaceae*, and they may be considered together.

Coriander was known by the Israelites during their captivity in Egypt, hence they likened the God-given manna in the desert to coriander seed (Exodus 16:31; Numbers 11:7). The round seed (actually fruit) is still used to give spicy flavouring to wine and food. The broad basal leaves are used in soups and salads but the upper leaves are too finely divided to be useful; rub over meat before roasting or use to flavour poultry stuffing.

Cumin (or cummin) has spicy seeds which were carefully tithed by the scribes and Pharisees in Jesus' time (Matthew 23:23). They are not to everyone's taste but are widely used in curry and kebabs, and baked in bread. Medicinally they are used for digestive disorders such as flatulence and diarrhoea; crushed coriander seeds relieve dizziness when inhaled.

Cultivation

Scatter the seeds of both plants in separate plots of open ground in early spring (or autumn in mild areas). Thin out the seedlings to 15cm (6in.) apart, keeping them free of weeds and moist around the roots. Collect the seeds when ripe before they fall to the ground, dry and store in airtight jars.

Species

Coriandrum sativum, coriander, S. Europe and N. Africa, 50cm (20in.), flowers white tinged pink (see pl. 11)

Cuminum cyminum, cumin, E. Mediterranean region, 45cm (18in.), flowers white (see fig. 5 and pl. 12)

Fig. 5. Cumin *Cuminum cyminum*, with flower and fruit.

Cucumber (*Cucumis*) and Melon (*Citrullus*)

Two refreshing fruits longed for by the Israelites wandering in the desert were melons and cucumbers: 'We remember the fish we used to eat in Egypt for nothing, the cucumbers, the melons …' (Numbers 11:5).

This melon was the water melon (*Citrullus lanatus*), the size of a football and with watery red flesh spotted with black seeds. The cucumber was the snake cucumber or musk melon (*Cucumis melo*) with long, grooved fruits. Both are trailing or sometimes climbing annuals, with yellow unisexual flowers like those of squash (pumpkin) and marrow, which are *Cucurbita* of American origin and therefore non-biblical.

Pl. 12. Cumin *Cuminum cyminum*, in an olive grove.

Cultivation

As these are tropical plants they can only be grown outside in warm countries or in greenhouses elsewhere. Alternatively, substitute the salad cucumber in a cold frame or the 'ridge' variety which is suitable for outdoors in temperate areas. Sow the seeds inside (15°C, 60°F) in early spring or outside after the danger of frost is past. If plants are raised in individual pots they can be planted out without disturbing the roots, but let them acclimatise to outdoor temperatures when they have developed five or six leaves before planting. They need rich soil with plenty of manure and make sure they are kept well watered. Let them trail along the ground or climb up a support. They produce a succession of moderate sized fruits from midsummer onwards providing they are regularly cut to encourage new flowers to develop.

Fig. 6. Water melon *Citrullus lanatus*, plant and fruit.

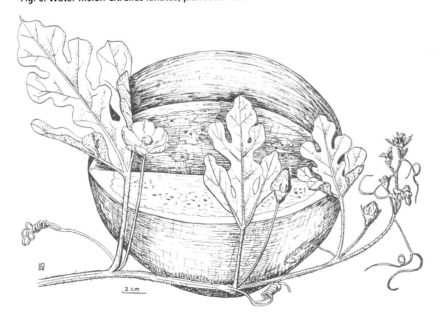

Species

Citrullus colocynthis, colocynth or wild gourds of the desert (2 Kings 4:39), a poisonous bitter fruit (perhaps the 'gall' of Matthew 27:34) (see also page 23)

C. lanatus (formerly known as *C. vulgaris*), water melon, tropical Africa (see fig. 6)

Cucumis melo, snake cucumber or musk melon, tropical Africa

C. sativa, cucumber, India reaching biblical lands rather late; the 'ridge cucumber' is a hardier cultivar

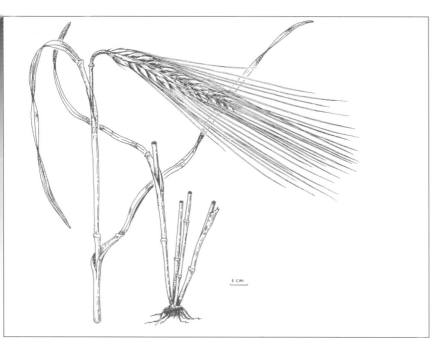

Fig.7. Common barley *Hordeum vulgare* (after Schiemann).

Barley (*Hordeum*)

Barley was the ordinary man's food in biblical times although barley loaves are coarser than those made of wheat. It grows in drier areas than wheat and has a shorter growing season. The scriptures often refer to barley as a crop (Exodus 9:31), as grain (Ezekiel 4:9) and as loaves (John 6:9). Harvesting barley was a familiar sight, with numerous labouring men followed by women gleaners (Ruth 1:22;2:3). Barley grain has long been used for malt production and beer brewing.

The barley plant is an annual grass growing 60-80cm (24-32in.) high. Its whiskery ears develop early and nod as they become heavy and mature. In a biblical garden they are decorative and may be cut for floral displays in the same way as wheat (page 26).

Cultivation

Sow barley grains 10mm (1/2in.) deep in dryish soil in an open situation during early spring. They can be scattered or sown in rows, or even in clumps in a flower border. The fruiting heads or ears turn yellow on ripening, rather earlier than wheat, in midsummer. The grains are set in spikelets with three flowers, but only one of these is fertile in the 'two-rowed barley', while all three are fertile in 'six-rowed barley'.

Pl. 13. Common barley *Hordeum vulgare.*

Species

Hordeum distichum, the two-rowed barley, originated in ancient times, like all barleys, in the Middle East, but is less frequently grown than six-rowed

H. spontaneum, wild barley, found throughout the Middle East as a serious weed of cultivation, is taller and more slender than cultivated barley and the ears are two-rowed

H. vulgare, common barley, the six-rowed barley (also known as *H. sativa* and *H. hexastichon*), the commonly grown cereal in temperate Europe (see fig. 7 and pl. 13)

Panicum miliaceum, proso millet, Asia, possibly the millet of Ezekiel 4:9 and more likely than another tall annual grass *Sorghum bicolor*, durra or sorghum (p. 25), from Africa which arrived later – it may have been there by New Testament times and could have been the 'hyssop' on which the sponge was raised to Jesus (John 19:29)

Pl. 14. Flax *Linum usitatissimum*.

Flax, Linen (*Linum*)

Linen is one of the world's oldest textiles and it is made from the fibres of the flax plant, *Linum usitatissimum*. The first biblical reference to linen occurs in Genesis (41:42) when Pharaoh, King of Egypt, dresses Joseph in fine linen and adorns him with gold for interpreting his dream. Egypt was famous for its flax (Exodus 9:31; Isaiah 19:9; Ezekiel 27:7 and 16), but it was grown in neighbouring countries, too. When Joshua sent two spies to the land of Canaan they were hidden from the King of Jericho's men under bundles of flax drying and blanching on the flat roof of a house (Joshua 2:1-6).

Linen fibres are prepared by 'retting' the flax stems, that is they are soaked in water until bacterial action separates the tough fibres from softer tissues. After combing, the fibres are spun into thread ready for weaving. The Israelite priests wore linen garments while officiating at the sacrifices (Leviticus 6:10; 16:4); the curtains in the Tabernacle and the Temple were also made of linen (Exodus 38:9 and 18; Luke 23:45). Elsewhere in the Bible white linen is depicted as symbolic of purity and righteousness (Ezekiel 44:17-18; Revelation 19:8 and 14).

Ancient Egyptian mummies were wrapped in linen after embalming. No doubt Joseph's body was treated in this way before being placed in the coffin (Genesis 50:26). The New Testament tells of Jesus' body being shrouded in linen prior to his burial in the rock-cut tomb at Calvary – 'with the spices in linen cloths, according to the burial custom of the Jews' (John 19:40) – and of how the cloths were left in the tomb at the resurrection (John 20:5-7).

Cultivation

Seeds rather thickly sown in ordinary garden soil in spring grow quickly and flower in 2-3 months when about 45 cm (18in.) high. The five blue petals of each flower soon fall, but new flower buds open in quick succession over a period of two or three weeks.

Species

Linum usitatissimum, true annual flax, Middle East. *L. humile* is smaller, cultivated in Ancient Egypt for its linseed oil (see fig. 8 and pl. 14)

Listed below are perennials of European origin which can be grown easily from seeds or propagated by cuttings. They are suited to a sunny rock garden and have flowers similar to the annual flax

Linum alpinum, alpine flax, 15cm (6in.) high

L. narbonense, up to 60cm (24in.) high

L. perenne, similar to the last

Fig. 8. Flax *Linum usitatissimum*, with fruit and seed.

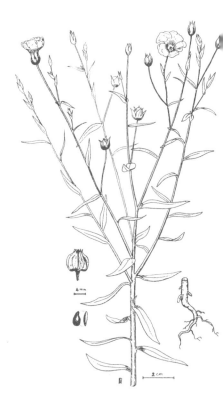

Pl. 15. Darnel *Lolium temulentum*.

best substitute is the Italian rye-grass (*Lolium multiflorum*) which is also an annual, or at most a biennial. Perennial rye-grass (*L. perenne*) is a common hay-grass in many temperate countries but it is hardly a suitable substitute for darnel.

Species

Lolium temulentum, darnel, Mediterranean region, parts of Europe, and has been introduced unintentionally into N. and S. America, S. Africa and Australia; annual. Care should be taken to avoid contamination of cereal crops and it may be illegal to grow it in some countries (see fig. 9 and pl. 15)

L. multiflorum, Italian rye-grass, a similar distribution, annual or biennial, 30-80cm (12-32in)

Fig. 9. Darnel *Lolium temulentum*, with enlarged spikelet.

Darnel, 'Tares' (*Lolium*)

A famous parable told by Jesus is that of the farmer who sowed good wheat in his field, but whose enemy afterwards secretly sowed a pernicious weed in the same ground. It was only when both the wheat and the weeds began to grow that the deed became known. The farm labourers wanted to pull up the weeds but the farmer said that in so doing they would pull up the wheat as well, so it was better to let them grow and separate them at harvest time (like sinners at the Day of Judgement!), when the weeds could be burnt and the wheat gathered into the barn (Matthew 13:24-30). This is often described as the Parable of the Tares, since the King James Version translated the Greek word *zizania* as 'tares', a kind of vetch. But the darnel grass (*Lolium temulentum*) is the weed in question and gives point to the parable. When wheat grain germinates, it is very similar to many other grasses, including the darnel. However, when the ears develop it is easy to tell them apart as the darnel is a smaller plant and the ears are more slender.

If darnel seeds are harvested and milled with wheat grains, sickness and even death are caused among those who eat bread made from the flour.

Darnel grows as an annual, 30-100cm (12-40in.) high with a slender ear, each of the chaffy flower groups ending in a short whisker (awn).

Cultivation

Darnel seed is not easily obtainable unless you collect it in the wild. Grains sown in spring grow well in any ground suitable for cereals. Like wheat and barley, darnel is an annual, so the

Black cumin, 'Fitches' (*Nigella*)

There is only one scriptural mention of black cumin, the 'fitches' of the Authorised King James Version: 'Dill is not threshed with a threshing-sledge, nor is a cartwheel rolled over [black] cummin' (Isaiah 28:27). The context shows that the oily black cumin seed must be treated carefully, unlike the hard grains of cereals which have to be threshed from the ear with sledges and cartwheels. The seeds are spicy and have long been used to flavour Middle Eastern food, and like poppy seeds are still sprinkled over bread.

Black cumin (*Nigella sativa*) is also known as 'nutmeg flower'. It is an annual herb, 30-45cm (12-18in.) high, with finely divided leaves. During the summer its mauve flowers are produced at the top of the stems, followed by the green capsules bearing horns, which are excellent in dried flower arrangements.

Cultivation

The popular garden flower love-in-a-mist is a very close relative of the black cumin and it is more decorative too. They are both similar in their cultivation and very easily grown. Seeds can be sown either in autumn or spring, the former producing earlier flowering plants, but in cold districts *N. sativa* should only be sown in spring. The soil conditions are not important, providing the situation is open and light. Thin out the seedlings 15cm (6in.) apart; if necessary they will transplant quite successfully. Collect the capsules before the seeds are shed, otherwise it will be impossible to find them on the ground.

Species

Nigella damascena, love-in-a-mist, southern Europe, up to 60cm (24in.) high, large blue flowers; an excellent substitute for *N. sativa* as seeds are readily available from garden shops and the flowers are more colourful

N. sativa, black cumin, nutmeg flower, North Africa, pale mauve flowers; the seeds are not easily obtainable, see previous entry for an alternative (see fig. 10 and pl. 16)

Fig. 10. Black cumin *Nigella sativa*, A plant, B nectary, C seed and fruit.

Pl. 16. Black cumin, Fitches *Nigella sativa*.

Pl. 17. Opium poppy *Papaver somniferum*.

Pl. 18. Hemlock *Conium maculatum*.

Species

Papaver rhoeas and similar species, corn or field poppy, Europe and introduced into temperate countries around the world, annual, up to 60cm (2ft), high (see figs. 6a, 11)

P somniferum, opium poppy, Asia, annual, up to 1m (3ft) high, flowers large and red or pale lilac-pink (see pl. 17)

Conium maculatum, hemlock, white umbelliferous annual, 1.5m (5ft), a bitter poisonous plant said to have killed Socrates. Similar cultivation to dill (p.14; see pl. 18)

Fig. 11. Corn poppy *Papaver rhoeas*.

Poppy (*Papaver*)

Poppies may be included in your Bible garden for two reasons. One is that scarlet field poppies are such a feature of the Mediterranean springtime that they were undoubtedly included in such passages as 'All people are grass, their constancy is like the flower of the field' (Isaiah 40:6) and 'All flesh is like grass and all its glory like the flower of grass. The grass withers, and the flower falls, but the word of the Lord endures for ever' (1 Peter 1: 24-25).

Secondly, the opium poppy may have provided the anodyne ('gall') in the vinegar offered to Jesus on the cross. 'They put a sponge full of wine on a branch of hyssop and held it to his mouth. When Jesus had received the wine, he said, "It is finished." Then he bowed his head and gave up his spirit' (John 19:29-30; Matthew 27:34). (See p. 18 for the colocynth gall, and below for hemlock.)

Poppy seeds are often scattered on to the surface of bread loaves or buns. This is the ornamental form and not the large capsule opium-yielding plant which should not be grown.

Cultivation

Nothing could be easier to grow than annual poppies. The seed scattered on the soil surface in spring where the plants are intended to bloom will grow without attention. As the scarlet poppies inhabit corn fields, why not have a few plants growing among your wheat and barley, where the flowers will make a very attractive feature? Opium poppy plants are taller, they have grey waxy leaves and are more suited to a herb garden. The single flowers are the wild type and more appropriate to your Bible garden than the horticulturists' double forms. To maintain succession snip off the dead flowers, which will also lessen the build up of seeds in your ground.

Thistles and Nettles (*Scolymus, Silybum, Urtica*)

Thistles, thorns and nettles feature throughout the Bible. In Genesis 3:17-18, we read of the curse of Adam, 'Cursed is the ground because of you . . . thorns and thistles it shall bring forth'; in Isaiah 34:13, 'Thorns shall grow over its strongholds, nettles and thistles in its fortresses'; and in the Parable of the Sower, 'Other seeds fell among thorns, and the thorns grew up and choked them' (Matthew 13:7).

Not many gardeners will wish to grow nettles in their Bible garden, but Mediterranean thistles can be very decorative, especially the golden thistles (*Scolymus hispanicus* and *S. maculatus*) and the holy thistle or milk thistle (*Silybum marianum*). The former are yellow and the latter pink. The large winter leaves of the milk thistle are beautifully white-veined. (See p. 50 for the woody thorny plants.)

Pl. 19. Syrian thistle *Notobasis syriaca*.

Cultivation

Although these plants come from the Mediterranean region they are quite hardy and the seeds can be sown in ordinary soil in early spring. If they are sown in their flowering position in autumn, thin out the seedlings to about 45cm (18in.) apart, or transplant the seedlings, when large enough to handle. They need an open sunny position. The golden thistle should have room to spread, the other thistles need a place where they will not overshadow smaller plants. Keep clear of paths where they could prick legs of visitors.

Species

Centaurea iberica, a star thistle, Mediterranean region, diffusely branched annual about 40cm (28in.) with long sharp thorns around the cream or pink flowerheads (see pl. 20)

Notobasis syriaca, Syrian thistle, Mediterranean region, large annual or biennial, flowers pink, flowering stems 1-1.5m (3-5ft) high from a winter rosette of white-veined leaves in second year; seed unlikely to be available commercially (see pl. 19)

Scolymus hispanicus, Spanish oyster or golden thistle, biennial or perennial, 60cm (2ft) high and nearly as wide, flowers yellow, summer; seeds occasionally available commercially

S. maculatus, spotted golden thistle, annual, similar to previous entry, with smaller flowers

Silybum marianum, holy or milk thistle, Mediterranean region, leaves and habit similar to *Notobasis*, flowering spring and summer, purple or white; seed available from specialist firms (see pl. 21)

Urtica urens, small stinging nettle, annual, throughout north temperate regions, probably occurring as a weed in your Bible garden whether you want it or not! Avoid perennial species which are too invasive

Urtica pilulifera, Roman nettle, Mediterranean region, annual

Pl. 20. Star thistle *Centaurea iberica*.

Pl. 21. Milk thistle *Silybum marianum*.

Pl. 22. Sorghum millet *Sorghum bicolor* in Yemen.

Sorghum millet, 'Hyssop' (*Sorghum*)

When the Lord Jesus Christ was crucified he was thirsty on the cross 'So they put a sponge full of the wine on a branch of hyssop and held it to his mouth' (John 19:29). Commentators have wondered what plant the 'hyssop' could have been since a bunch of marjoram twigs (see p. 38) would be unsuitable. Matthew actually says that a 'reed' was used and this is much more likely. Such a stick could have been from a common reed or giant reed (p. 75) but some commentators suggest the reed-like stem of the sorghum cereal. This is grown in warm countries as an annual crop about the height of a person with a nodding cluster of grains at its head. It was introduced into lowland Palestine in New Testament times.

Cultivation

Probably the easiest way to obtain sorghum seeds is from a pet shop. Sow them in garden soil in a very warm position in full sunlight where they can grow up to their full height. Though the plants may not mature their grains, sorghum is worth growing as an ornamental grass at the back of the bed.

Species

Sorghum bicolor (*S. vulgare*) millet, dura, Guinea corn, tropical Africa, annual, up to 5m (16ft) high (see pl. 22)

Wheat (*Triticum*)

Wheat and barley are the 'corn' or 'grain' frequently mentioned in the Bible, and not to be confused with Indian corn or maize of the New World. It was wheat which featured in Pharaoh's dream of seven years' plenty ('Seven ears of grain, plump and good, were growing on one stalk'), and seven years' famine ('Seven empty ears, thin and blighted by the east wind') (Genesis 41:5-6). So Joseph gathered wheat into barns in Egypt, where his brothers came during the famine (Genesis 42). Cereal offerings to the Lord had to be of fine wheat flour (Leviticus 2:1-16), and in the New Testament we read the Parable of the Sower (Matthew 13:3-9), and also how Jesus likened himself to a grain of wheat – 'If it dies, it bears much fruit' (John 12:24).

Pl. 23. Threshing in the traditional manner, near Nazareth, Israel.

Pl. 24. Winnowing in fields near Nazareth.

Pl. 25. Emmer wheat *Triticum dicoccum*.

Fig. 12. : Emmer wheat *Triticum dicoccum* (after Schiemann).

In Old Testament times the wheat grown was emmer wheat (*Triticum dicoccum*) which is a robust grass 1-1.5m (3-5ft) tall with its ears covered in long whiskers (awns). Later on another one, which is popularly known as 'bread wheat' (*T. aestivum*), came into general cultivation. This is the wheat grown for flour nowadays; it is not as tall as emmer and usually is without awns.

Cultivation

Wheat is best sown in autumn in order to give it a long growing season. However, early spring sowing is quite satisfactory for a Bible garden. Rather than sow broadcast, place the grains close together in lines over a hoe width apart to enable weeding to take place (unless, like me, you actively favour the idea of encouraging poppies and other weeds in the corn).

The soil should be enriched with manure or compost during preparation. When the tall wheat comes into ear, it may need supporting with sticks and string to prevent the stalks bending over. Birds can be troublesome as they eat the ripening grain, and only by completely netting the plot can this be prevented; however, such steps are seldom necessary. The yellow straw and ears are very decorative in the garden or can be picked for dried floral displays. In wet weather, however, mildew discolours the ears, so it is advisable to collect them as soon as ripe. Seed for the next sowing should be set aside in a labelled envelope. In the first place grains can usually be found in a harvested cornfield, or in birdseed mixture, or even obtained from a friendly healthfood shopkeeper.

Species

Triticum aestivum (also known as *T. vulgare*), the bread wheat, commonly grown for flour today, and easily obtainable (see fig. 12 right)

T. dicoccum, emmer wheat, originated in E. Mediterranean region, seldom cultivated now (see fig. 12 left and pl. 25)

T. durum, hard or macaroni wheat, derived from the above, still widely cultivated in the Mediterranean area for pasta

Beans and Peas (*Vicia, Cicer, Lens, Pisum*)

Collectively these are known as 'legumes' or pulses, important protein vegetables in the pea family *Leguminosae*. Esau sold his birthright to his brother Jacob for a bowl of red lentil soup (Genesis 25:29-34); and later broad beans and lentils were included in the gifts brought to King David when he fled from Absalom's rebellion (2 Samuel 17:28). Two more legumes, chick pea and garden pea, also come from the Middle East and perhaps were among the vegetables ('pulse') on which David and his countrymen fed during their exile in Babylon, instead of eating Nebuchadnezzar's rich delicacies (Daniel 1:12 and 16) – and, 'At the end of ten days it was observed that they appeared better and fatter than all the young men who had been eating the royal rations.'

Cultivation

Legumes are popular in our vegetable gardens and easily grown. While broad beans and garden peas need rich limy soil, chick peas and lentils prefer light sandy soil; all should be grown in open situations. Provide broad beans with plenty of space, sowing the large seeds 15cm (6in.) apart during the winter or early spring; sow peas a little later in close rows; lentils and chick peas can be scattered when there is no danger of frost. In practice, broad beans and peas are most likely to be included in biblical gardens as their seeds are readily available and they tolerate cool conditions; chick peas and lentils do better in countries with warm dry climates. Broad beans attract blackfly which multiply rapidly on the young shoots unless they are sprayed and the tops pinched out after several clusters of flowers have developed: early planting also helps to control blackfly. Peas usually require sticks for support, but they are unnecessary for the other legumes.

Pl. 26. Broad bean pods *Vicia faba*.

Species

Cicer arietinum, chick pea, Middle East, annual, 30cm (12in.) high, forming a tangle with small tendrils; flowers white; pods with few seeds, each shaped like the head of a chicken or hawk – they are cooked or ground into a delicious paste, called hummus, and eaten with olive oil and bread

Lens esculenta, lentil, Middle East, annual, 15-45cm (6-18in.) high, almost erect, tendril at end of each pinnate leaf; pale blue flowers, very small; pods usually one-seeded; pull up the plants when yellow, and collect seeds for soup or paste

Pisum sativum, garden pea, Europe, annual climber, 60-120cm (24-48in.) high; flowers usually white, sometimes red, especially in Mediterranean regions; cook the seeds young, but allow those required for sowing to mature; many varieties available

Vicia faba (*Faba vulgaris*), broad bean, Middle East, erect annual, 100cm (40in.) high, flowers white with black spot; the thick hairy pods are about 15cm (6in.) long – either cook the whole pod when very young or the large seeds while still tender. The small ancient bean should be called the horse bean (*V. faba* var. *equina*) (see fig. 13 and pl. 26)

Fig. 13. Broad bean *Vicia faba*, with flower, pod and bean.

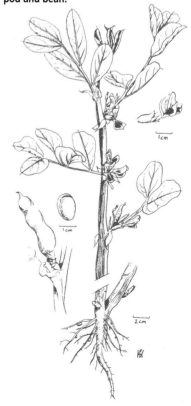

2
Perennials

Pl. 27. Mandrake, *Mandragora officinarum*, in flower.

Herbaceous perennials live for many years, dying down at the end of each season. At that time of year they may be lifted, split and replanted. This enables you to reduce the size of a large clump, to propagate the plants, or to dig over the ground where they have grown, clearing any noxious weeds and manuring it.

Included in this group are the plants with corms (*Anemone*, *Crocus*) and bulbs (*Lilium*, *Narcissus*, *Ornithogalum* and *Tulipa*) which need special treatment as indicated in the notes on cultivation.

Planting
Before planting perennials remember that they are likely to be there for some years and they will spread sideways during that time. Remember, also, that some will be shorter than others and that they will flower at different times – you can compensate for this by mixing them with annuals and shrubs in the planting scheme.

Manure or compost should be dug into the ground together with some bone-meal for lasting fertilising effect. Make sure that the soil is free from perennial weeds such as couch grass and bindweed, otherwise they will find refuge among the new plantings. Mulching with weed-free compost helps to retain moisture around the roots, especially in light soil.

Propagation of perennials is usually simply by dividing the clumps, as indicated above. Cuttings and seeds can also be used. Perennials with tap roots (*Cichorium, Ferula, Mandragora*) are best propagated by growing from seeds. Bulbs grown from seeds will take several years to reach flowering size.

Anemone
(*Anemone*)

Whether the poppy anemone is the 'lily of the field' that was more richly clothed than Solomon in his glory (Matthew 6:28-29; Luke 12:27-28) is never likely to be resolved, but this colourful wild flower is such a feature of the Holy Land during early spring that a biblical garden would hardly be complete without it. It is a perennial with short divided leaves and single large flowers on stalks about 30cm (12in.) high. The flowers are scarlet, blue, purple, or even white and they are well known as cut flowers that last a long time in water. Some similar alternative Mediterranean species are listed below.

Cultivation

The dried corms are about 10mm (1/2in.) in diameter and if planted in autumn will flower in spring, while those planted in spring flower in summer. Plant them 50mm (2in.) deep and 75mm (3in.) apart with the point downwards in well-drained and cultivated soil in a sunny position. In spite of the fact that wild plants flourish in rocky hillsides, in cultivation they do

Fig.14. Poppy anemone *Anemone coronaria.*

Pl. 29. Asian buttercup *Ranunculus asiaticus.*

need to be well fed with compost. They can be grown as pot plants, too. Although the plants may last for years outdoors, if they are subject to too much moisture in the summer they will rot away; hence lifting, drying and replanting the corms will ensure their continuation. In cold regions protect the plants in frosty weather by covering with glass or straw.

Species

Anemone coronaria, poppy anemone, wind flower, Israel and neighbouring countries (see fig. 14 and pls. 3 and 28); the double-flowered cultivar usually known as 'De Caen' is not as suitable as the wild type singles; alternatively try one of the following substitute species:

A. fulgens, probably a hybrid between *A. pavonina* and *A. hortensis*, flowers scarlet, easily cultivated

A. hortensis, southern Europe, flowers pink or mauve

A. pavonina, France to Turkey, flowers scarlet, pink or purple, usually with a whitish centre

Ranunculus asiaticus, Turk's cap (double) or Asian buttercup (see pl. 29)

Pl. 28. Poppy anemone *Anemone coronaria.*

Wormwood (*Artemisia*)

The bitterness of wormwood is referred to in several scriptural passages, for example, 'He has filled me with bitterness, he has glutted me with wormwood' (Lamentations 3:15) and, 'The name of the star is Wormwood. A third of the waters became Wormwood, and many died from the water, because it was made bitter' (Revelation 8:11).

Most species of wormwood have grey, fragrant foliage and make attractive garden plants. The Middle Eastern species may not be available or suitable as they are desert plants but others

Pl. 30. Wormwood *Artemisia arborescens* planted in St George's Bible Garden, Jerusalem.

Fig. 15. Wormwood *Artemisia herba-alba*, with flowers.

would make good substitutes. They are mostly perennial herbs or small shrubs with insignificant flowers in spite of their belonging to the daisy family (*Compositae*).

Cultivation

Propagation is by division of clumps in spring or by cuttings taken during the summer. Plant where the grey foliage will be seen to the best effect in full sun, in ordinary garden soil, and they will thrive in dry situations, too.

Species

Artemisia absinthium, absinthe, common wormwood, Europe, perennial, 45cm (18in.)

A. arborescens, S. Europe, shrubby stems up to 1m (3ft) high (see pl. 30)

A. herba-alba, Middle East, desert undershrub, probably the one referred to in the Bible (see fig. 15)

A. judaica, Holy Land, an annual species also probably used in biblical times; seeds unlikely to be available commercially

A. maritima, sea wormwood, western coast of Europe and across Asia in salty places, low-growing perennial with white foliage

Tragacanth, 'Gum' (*Astragalus*)

The Ishmaelites who were heading southwards to Egypt along the trade routes of the Fertile Crescent 'coming from Gilead with their camels bearing gum, balm, and resin' (Genesis 37:25, see also Genesis 43:11), would have been carrying local products from the north, rather than tropical products with the same names. I have identified the 'balm' with mastic from terebinth (p. 88) or storax (p. 48) and 'resin' from rock-rose (p. 45), which leaves us with the 'gum'. There is little doubt that this was the well-known gum tragacanth obtained from the lower stems of *Astragalus gummifer*, *A. bethlehemicus* and related species. They are members of the pea family (Leguminosae which grow like spiny pin-cushions on the dry, stony hillsides of the Middle East. When collectors cut off the stems where they join the tap-root the gum exudes under its own pressure. Since these species are unlike-

Pl. 31. Tragacanth *Astragalus bethlehemicus* on Mt Sinai.

ly to be available for your garden, suitable alternatives need to be chosen. The genus *Astragalus* contains hundreds of species with different life-forms, including some with a cushion habit (e.g. *A. angustifolius*) which may be available from specialist nurseries.

Cultivation

Tragacanths need an open, sunny position in well-drained stony soil. Seeds may take a long time to germinate, and the plants resent root disturbance, so whether they are raised from seeds or bought from a nursery make sure that they are moved as little as possible.

Species

Astragalus bethlehemicus, gum tragacanth, Palestine, Sinai, spiny cushion under-shrub (see pl. 31)

A. gummifer, gum tragacanth, S.W. Asia, spiny cushion under-shrub

Pl. 32. Chicory bitter herb *Cichorium intybus*.

Chicory and Bitter Herbs (*Cichorium etc.*)

When the people of Israel were about to escape from Egypt for the Promised Land, they ate their first Passover meal: roast meat with unleavened bread and bitter herbs as a reminder of harsh experiences (Exodus 12:8; Numbers 9:11). They would have plucked whatever leaves were available, although today Jews celebrate their Passover (*Seder*) meal with bitter herbs such as chicory, lettuce, eryngo, horseradish and sow-thistle, or parsley as a substitute for them all. Chicory leaves, as well as endive, are used as a salad while the long roots are roasted, ground and mixed with coffee. Lettuce is too well known to require description but it is worth mentioning that the ancient form of it resembled the present day Cos variety with erect leaves, not the rounded cabbage type. Eryngo is related to the sea-holly and very prickly in fields; only its youngest leaves are edible. Horseradish is grown for its spicy white root which may be lifted, cut and replanted as wanted. Sow-thistle grows wild and its leaves may be boiled as spinach.

Cultivation

Sow chicory seeds from spring to early summer and thin seedlings to 20cm (8in.) apart. Light soil in an open situation is best. The plants will grow like lettuce but the following year will attain a height of about 2m (6ft) producing each morning a succession of delightful blue flowers about 4cm (11/2in.) across. Lettuce seeds

Fig. 16. Chicory *Cichorium intybus*, with a flower and seed.

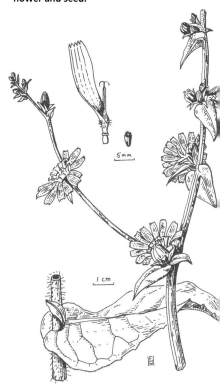

can be sown from early spring to mid-summer and any plants not used for salad will bolt, that is produce a mass of small yellow flowers on a leafy stem about 60cm (24in.) high. Parsley seeds are often slow to germinate unless soaked in hot water; keep the plants moist or they will bolt.

Species

Armoracia rusticana (*Cochlearia armoracia*), horseradish, Europe in waste places, perennial, tufted coarse leaves 0.5m (11/2ft), white flowers late spring

Cichorium intybus, chicory, Europe, hardy perennial; basal leaves have milky juice providing a bitter taste (see fig. 16 and pl. 32)

C. pumilum, dwarf chicory, Mediterranean region, perennial often forming rosettes on the soil surface, yet growing to 30cm (12in.) or more when not trampled or grazed; seeds may be difficult to obtain commercially

Eryngium creticum, eryngo, Mediterranean region. The garden ornamental perennials *E. amethystinum* and *E. tripartitum* could be grown instead

Lactuca sativa, lettuce, S. Europe and W. Asia, tender annual. For the Cos variety see note above

Petroselinium crispum, parsley, S. Europe and Asia Minor, biennial

Sonchus oleraceus, sow-thistle, Europe and introduced widely elsewhere, annual weed with rosette of leaves; stem 40-60cm (16-24in) high; flowers yellow

Saffron crocus (*Crocus*)

The Song of Solomon is a rich mine for the mention of spices and other plants: 'Your shoots are an orchard of pomegranates with all choicest fruits, henna with nard, nard and saffron, calamus and cinnamon, with all trees of frankincense, myrrh and aloes, with all chief spices' (4:13-14, RSV). The saffron

Pl. 33. Saffron crocus, *Crocus sativus*.

referred to is a yellow powder obtained by collecting and grinding the styles of *Crocus sativus*. Hence this has always been an expensive substance which is still used for dyeing foodstuffs yellow and imparting a subtle flavour.

The saffron crocus is similar to many others in the genus with purple flowers and yellow anthers, but with large orange-red styles. In autumn the rounded corms produce flowers together with very narrow leaves. For a biblical garden one could substitute one of the purple- or blue-flowered species listed below. In fact, the NRSV rendering of the prophecy in Isaiah 35:1 reads, 'The desert shall rejoice and blossom; like the crocus it shall blossom abundantly' (other versions read 'rose'; see also Song of Solomon 2:1) so it is reasonable to include crocus species in your garden.

Cultivation

Most species of crocus thrive in ordinary well-drained garden soil and they are best planted 8cm (3in.) deep and 5cm (2in.) apart at random or in small clumps. The saffron, however, needs special treatment, or it will fail to flower and die away. You should prepare the patch where it is to grow by digging out about 30cm (12in.) deep; fill up with rich, well-manured soil and plant the corms deeply. All crocuses are best lifted in summer, when the

leaves have died down, and replanted as soon as possible, especially saffron and other autumn-flowering species. Corms are obtainable from nurserymen, propagation being from offsets or by seeds which take about three years to reach the flowering stage.

Fig. 17. Saffron *Crocus sativus*.

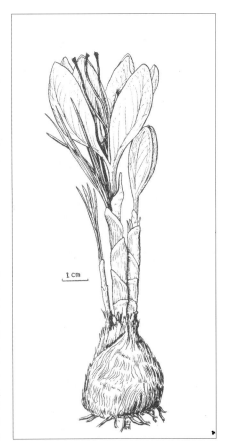

1 cm

Species

Crocus nudiflorus, autumn crocus, Pyrenees of France and Spain, very similar to saffron and also used like it, with purple flowers but leaves developing later

C. kotschyanus (or *C. zonatus*), Syria, pale lilac in autumn

C. sativus, the true saffron, probably originally from Greece, flowering in autumn (see fig. 17 and pl. 33)

C. speciosus, similar to *C. nudiflorus*

Other *Crocus* species and hybrids widely cultivated could be used to ornament the garden

Pl. 34. Giant Fennel *Ferula communis.*

Giant Fennel, 'Galbanum' (*Ferula*)

One of the unusual spices used in the Old Testament rites was galbanum, a constituent of the Holy Incense which was burnt as a perfume in the Tabernacle (Exodus 30:34). Nowadays it is not used at all and the plant from which it came, a giant fennel (*Ferula galbaniflua*), grows only on the dry hillsides of Iran. For a Bible garden, therefore, it is necessary to provide a substitute plant and for this I suggest the common giant fennel (*Ferula communis*) or even culinary fennel (*Foeniculum vulgare*).

These are tall perennials in the parsley family, *Umbelliferae* or *Apiaceae*, with umbels of yellow flowers. They have deep taproots and finely divided leaves, and where the leaves meet the stem there is an inflated sheath which is particularly characteristic of the *Ferula* species.

Cultivation

All these plants are hardy perennials easily raised from seed. The giant fen-nel seeds may need to be collected from wild plants and they should be sown as soon as ripe, but culinary fennel bought commercially can wait until spring. Thin or plant out in ordinary soil in a sunny position where the decorative leaves can be seen, allowing sufficient room for them to spread as they may take several years to flower. Culinary fennel, however, is a short-lived perennial and may even flower the first year. The fragrant gums are obtained from notches in the roots; fennel leaves and seeds can be used in cooking and for sauces.

Species

Ferula communis, giant fennel, Mediterranean region, 1-2m (3-6ft) high, flowering in spring (see pl. 34)

Ferula galbaniflua, galbanum, Iran, the true plant, but unobtainable commercially (see fig. 18)

Foeniculum vulgare, fennel, Mediterranean region, 1-1.5m (3-5ft) high, flowering in summer; cv 'Purpurea' has purple stems and foliage; the Florentine fennel is grown for its bulbous base as a vegetable.

Fig. 18. Galbanum *Ferula galbaniflua*, with fruits.

Lily (*Lilium*)

There are several references to lilies in the Bible but they do not necessarily refer to the true lily. However, it is quite likely that the white or Madonna lily was the plant in Hosea's prophecy: 'I will be like the dew to Israel; he shall blossom like the lily' (14:5). At any rate there is a long-standing tradition that this is a biblical plant.

It occurs very rarely nowadays on Mount Carmel and the hills further north but is well-known in cultivation. Its common name, Madonna lily, refers to the fact that because of its whiteness Roman Catholic artists depicted it as symbolic of the Virgin Mary. Its bulb is the usual lily type composed of overlapping pale yellow scales and not concentric like an onion; its short basal leaves persist during the winter. In spring the leafy stem begins to grow and when it is about 1m (3ft) high, several flower buds develop in

Pl. 35. Madonna lily *Lilium candidum*.

the upper part. The large flowers open in succession during the summer, pure white and beautifully scented.

Cultivation

As the bulbs are leafy in autumn and winter, they must be planted while dormant in summer with the tops only just below the surface. They tolerate limy soil and they should be in a sheltered situation in full sun. Place them where the white flowers will show up against a dark background and where you can be sure of taking advantage of their fragrance. Lilies are often attacked by a virus which withers the leaves and stunts the plants; infected plants should be burnt and new ones obtained.

Species

Lilium candidum, white Madonna lily; if this actual species cannot be obtained or grown, another white species may be substituted, such as *L. regale*, the royal lily, for outside cultivation, or *L. longiflorum*, the white trumpet lily, for a cool greenhouse or a warm sheltered position outdoors (see fig. 19 and pl. 35)

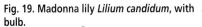

Fig. 19. Madonna lily *Lilium candidum*, with bulb.

Mallows (*Malva, Atriplex*)

There is an obscure item of tasteless food mentioned in Job 6:6, variously translated 'white of egg' (King James Version, New International Version), or 'mallows' (New English Bible, New Revised Standard Version). Professor Michael Zohary considered it, on linguistic grounds, to be a mallow (*Malva*) or hollyhock (*Althaea* or *Alcea*).

One of the mallows of the Holy Land, as well as throughout Europe and North America, is the common mallow, *Malva sylvestris*. It is a roadside perennial, often seen dwarfed by mowing or grazing, with lateral branches up to 40cm (16in.) long. The rounded basal leaves are up to 10cm (4in.) in diameter and persist all year round, while the smaller stem leaves are quite deeply lobed. The leaves may be collected and cooked lightly as a mucilaginous spinach or a soup thickener; skin ointments and cough medi-

Pl. 36. Shrubby orache *Atriplex halimus*.

cines can also be prepared from them. Mallow flowers are large and decorative, mauve or pink, throughout the summer and well worth growing in a biblical garden; hollyhocks need to be placed at the back because of their height.

The 'mallow' mentioned later in Job (30:4) – where it is gathered by starving men from waste-ground – is obviously a desert plant, most likely the shrubby orache *Atriplex halimus*. This occurs commonly in salty places by the Dead Sea and along the coasts of Europe. Standing over 1m (3ft) high, it has a tangle of silvery grey twigs and leaves, and small greenish flowers in terminal clusters.

Cultivation

Mallows and hollyhocks are best raised from seeds sown in autumn or early spring where they are intended to flower in the same or the following year. Thin out to give them room to develop, up to 1m (3ft) apart for hollyhocks. Mulch and keep moist during summer. Perennial species can be propagated from cuttings taken in summer. They are susceptible to rust fungus which may be treated with benzeate spray.

Plant shrubby orache in autumn and prune in spring if necessary. It succeeds in light soil near the sea and if frosted usually recovers by producing new shoots. In cold countries it should be pot-grown in a cool greenhouse and placed outside in summer. Propagate by cuttings in summer.

Species

Althaea rosea, hollyhock, China, readily available; may be substituted for the wild *Alcea setosa* of the Holy Land; over 2m (6ft) tall (pl. 5)

Atriplex canescens, grey salt bush, N.W. America, 1-2m (3-6ft), grey-leaved; could be used as a garden substitute for shrubby orache

A. halimus, Mediterranean, shrubby orache or tree purslane (see pl. 36)
Halimione portulacoides (or *Atriplex*

portulacoides), sea purslane, N. Africa and Europe, salt marshes, low shrub with grey leaves; could be used as a substitute for shrubby orache

Malva sylvestris, common mallow, hardy biennial best grown as an annual, flowers purple

M. alcea and *M. moschata*, musk mallow, Europe, similar to common mallow, with deeply cut leaves and pink flowers

Mandrake (*Mandragora*)

When Jacob's son Reuben brought back to his mother Leah mandrake fruits that he had found in the harvest field, his father's other wife, Rachel, pleaded for them but was sharply rebuffed by Leah (Genesis 30:14-16). Why? Because of the association of mandrakes with an ancient fertility cult, which appears again in the Song of Solomon (7:13).

The mandrake is a member of the Deadly Nightshade family. Its taproot is said to resemble the human form. Among its rosette of large leaves during the autumn or early spring, nestles a cluster of pale mauve flowers producing yellow egg-like fruits which are fragrant and feature in folklore.

Fig. 20. Mandrake *Mandragora officinarum* with root, flower and fruits.

Pl. 37. Mandrake *Mandragora officinarum* in fruit.

Cultivation

Seeds are occasionally available from specialist firms, or you may be able to collect the fruits often seen around ruins and in waste ground in the eastern Mediterranean region. The seeds sprout readily in warm conditions but it is difficult to prevent slugs and snails eating the seedlings, so it is best to sow a few seeds in a pot and plant outside without disturbing the tap-root.

Species

Mandragora officinarum, mandrake, E. Mediterranean region, perennial (see fig. 20 and pls. 27, 37)

M. autumnalis, a name sometimes given to the autumn-flowering plants

Mint (*Mentha*)

No herb garden is complete without mint – and evidently this was true in New Testament times too, since it was one of those herbs mentioned by Jesus (Matthew 23:23; Luke 11:42). You probably already grow mint as a culinary herb, and can label it appropriately for your Bible garden. The choice of species is not important.

Cultivation

Mint grows best in well-manured, moist soil, but any good garden soil in an open or semi-shaded situation is suitable. As the long underground rhizomes are invasive, precautions should be taken to ensure that they do not smother their neighbours: grow them beside a path or in a sink, for example.

Species

Mentha longifolia, horsemint, Europe and W. Asia, the authentic species, 80cm (32in.) high; can be used like spearmint (see below). Arabs use it for tea (see fig. 21 and pl. 38)

M. piperita, peppermint, Europe and W. Asia, 30-60cm (12-24in.) high, with purple stems; not suitable for cooking, but good for herbal tea

M. spicata, spearmint, Europe, 60cm (24in.), the popular mint of British gardens; many varieties and hybrids. It is often used for mint sauce with roast lamb, and a leaf or two is boiled with new potatoes

Pl. 38. Horsemint, *Mentha longifolia*.

Fig. 21. Horsemint *Mentha longifolia*, with a flower.

Narcissus (*Narcissus*)

Although a great deal of discussion has centred on the identity of the biblical lily, various authors have come to different conclusions. Some believe that the polyanthus narcissus (*Narcissus tazetta*) was the plant mentioned by Solomon: 'I am a rose of Sharon, a lily of the valleys. As a lily among brambles, so is my love among maidens' (Song of Solomon 2:1-2). Others consider it to be the biblical rose!

This is a beautiful bulb growing wild in moist valleys and hills of the Holy Land where it flowers as early as November in the cool rainy winter. By the time spring comes the narrow leaves have stored up food in the bulb and wither away before the summer begins. The flower-head is composed of a cluster of white flowers each having a short orange-yellow trumpet (or corona). The scent is as much a joy as the colour of the flowers.

Fig. 22. Polyanthus narcissus *Narcissus tazetta* cultivar, with bulbs.

Pl. 39. Wild polyanthus narcissus *Narcissus tazetta*.

Cultivation

This narcissus is a favourite garden plant in temperate countries where it flowers early in the spring and is a useful cut flower. Popular cultivars are readily available, although the wild form may be more difficult to find commercially. Like the daffodil and its relatives, the polyanthus narcissus requires cool, moist rooting conditions. Plant the bulbs in late summer 7-10cm (3in.) deep in heavy soils, 15cm (6in.) in light soils, in irregular clumps where they can stay for several years before lifting, splitting and replanting. A little bonemeal at planting time is helpful, but not manure. Let the leaves die down completely before clearing them, otherwise flowering will be inhibited. Bulbs are easily grown indoors in well-drained pots.

Species

Narcissus tazetta, polyanthus narcissus, Europe to Japan, 50cm (20in.) high, the true species with white and orange-yellow flowers. The following named cultivars are derived from it and its relations: 'Paper White', pure white double flowers without the corona, very early flowering; 'Soleil d'Or', all-yellow single flowers that are extremely fragrant (see fig. 22 and pl. 39)

Hyacinthus orientalis, wild hyacinth, E. Mediterranean region, well-known fragrant bulbous plant easily grown indoors or outside; sometimes considered to be one of the biblical 'lilies'; the wild plant is blue flowered.

Tulipa (See p. 42).

Marjoram, 'Hyssop' (*Origanum*)

This is the biblical 'hyssop', at least in several of the verses where the word is used (in others it refers to sorghum – see p. 25 – and caper – see p. 81). A bunch of 'hyssop' was used for sprinkling blood on the door lintels and posts at the time of Passover (Exodus 12:22) and during the sacrifices in the Tabernacle (Leviticus 14:4,6,52; Numbers 19:6,18). The hairy, wiry stems of this mint-like plant, *Origanum syriacum*, would be suitable for such a purpose. It grows on rocks in dry country in the Holy Land. A suitable substitute for a biblical garden is pot marjoram, *O. onites*, which has a similar appearance with small heads of white flowers. Another option is sweet marjoram, *O. majorana*, the well-known herb which normally has purple flowers, but there is a white variety. Nowadays 'hyssop' is applied to an entirely different garden plant, *Hyssopus officinalis* of S. Europe.

Cultivation

Both pot and sweet marjoram require good soil in an open situation. Their tiny seeds can be sown in a frame in early spring, covering the seeds very lightly and transplanting the seedlings outdoors when they are large enough to handle, or sown outside in warmer weather. As the plants are perennial it is possible to propagate them by division, which should be done in any case every three or four years. In cool regions they may not survive the winter and it is best to consider them as annuals. If you wish to use them for culinary purposes, gather the shoots in midsummer just before flowering time, and dry them in a shady place before storing.

Fig. 23. Syrian marjoram *Origanum syriacum*, with a flower.

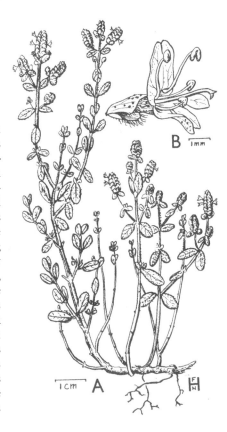

Pl. 41. Syrian marjoram, biblical hyssop, *Origanum syriacum.*

Pl. 42. Dove's dung, *Ornithogalum narbonense* subsp. *brachystachys.*

Species

Origanum majorana (also called *Majorana hortensis*), sweet or knotted marjoram, N. Africa, 30-60cm (12-24in.), rather tender half-hardy perennial

O. onites, pot marjoram, Mediterranean region, 30cm (12in.)

O. syriacum (also called *O. maru*), E. Mediterranean region, 45-100cm (18-40in.), rather tender, the biblical species (see fig. 23 and pl. 41)

O. vulgare, common or wild marjoram, Europe, is a hardy, vigorous grower with purple (or white) flowers in heads. It could be used as a substitute for the biblical species in colder climates

Star-of-Bethlehem, 'Dove's dung' (*Ornithogalum*)

There is a curious and puzzling biblical reference to dove's dung being sold for a high price in Samaria during a famine when Benhadad, King of Syria, was besieging the city (2 Kings 6:25).

Some authors consider this 'dove's dung' to be the bulb of a small plant now often called star-of-Bethlehem (*Ornithogalum*). It grows so profusely on the hills of Samaria that the white flowers look like bird droppings on the ground.

Most species of *Ornithogalum* are poisonous but there is an exception – *O. narbonense* which grows in the Holy Land. It has a spike of white flowers in springtime. The leaves of some species have a white midrib and the exteriors of the white flowers are striped with green, making them difficult to see during dull weather, but they open wide in sunshine.

Cultivation

The small white bulbs are easily grown in ordinary garden soil. Plant them 5cm (2in.) deep in the autumn, in a sunny position. They increase quite readily forming a clump which may be used for propagating them.

Species

Ornithogalum narbonense, E. Mediterranean region, the authentic subspecies is *brachystachys*, 15-30cm (6-12in.) high, flowers white; obtainable from specialist firms, otherwise the following are ready available as substitutes (see fig. 24 and pl. 42).

O. nutans, Europe, 20-30cm (8-12in.) high, nodding green flowers

O. tenuifolium, Europe, more slender than the next species

O. umbellatum, Europe, Star-of-Bethlehem, 30cm (12in.), erect white flowers in a flat-topped head

Fig. 24. Dove's dung *Ornithogalum narbonense* subsp. *brachystachys.*

Rue (*Ruta*)

There is only one mention of this aromatic plant in the Bible, namely Jesus' attack on the religious observances of the scribes and Pharisees (Luke 11:42). In New Testament times presumably rue was cultivated along with mint, dill and other herbs, although wild rue (*Ruta chalepensis*) could have been gathered on the hillsides without difficulty.

Wild rue is a tough little shrub straggling about and growing up to 60cm (2ft) high, with much divided leaves that are highly fragrant – pinch a leaf and you have the odour on your fingers for the rest of the day. During the summer it produces numerous greenish-yellow flowers, each having four fringed petals. In the similar and more familiar common rue of southern Europe, *R. graveolens*, the petals are not fringed. This is the species often grown in herb and flower gardens but it is too strong to be used much as a culinary herb. It is said to have medicinal use against insect stings, and people thought it warded off disease.

Top: Pl. 43. Wild rue *Ruta chalepensis*; bottom: pl. 44. Common rue *Ruta graveolens*.

Fig. 25. Common rue *Ruta graveolens*, with a flower.

Cultivation

Rue is a decorative evergreen, easily grown and ideal for filling in gaps in your Bible garden. Branches torn off and inserted wherever you have a space are almost sure to root, or new plants may be raised from seeds. It tolerates poor dry soil and a surprising amount of shade (although it may not flower). Trim in summer to encourage compact growth, but bear in mind that some people find they produce a skin rash or blistering, so handle carefully.

Species

Ruta chalepensis, wild rue, Mediterranean region including Israel (see pl. 43)

R. graveolens, common rue (Shakespeare's 'herb of grace'), S. Europe; cv 'Jackman's Blue' has decorative blue-green foliage (see fig. 25 and pl. 44)

Sage (*Salvia*)

When Moses led the People of Israel through the Sinai Desert, God gave him not only the Ten Commandments, but also the instructions for the meeting tent they were to construct, frequently known as the Tabernacle. Minute details were provided, including specifications for the great lampstand of pure gold, the *Menorah* in Hebrew. 'The base and the shaft of the lampstand were made of hammered work; its cups, its calyxes and its petals were of one piece with it. There were six branches going out of its sides' (Exodus 37:17-18). This kind of branching is very plant-like, and the prototype is generally considered to be the wild Judean sage, *Salvia judaica*. It is a perennial of dry country, with blue flowers, growing 40-80cm (16-32in.)

tall. No doubt the fragrant leaves were also used for flavouring, as are different species of sage elsewhere today.

Cultivation

As *S. judaica* is virtually impossible to obtain, save by collecting seed from the wild plants, other species will need to be substituted. A good alternative is the field clary, *S. pratensis*, which has lampstand-like inflorescences up to 1m (3ft) high. The common sage, *S. officinalis*, in spite of its being rather shrubby, forms a rounded plant 60-100cm (2-3ft) high. It may be raised from seed sown under glass in March and planted out in May, or by pulling off the side shoots from an old bush in spring and inserting them in moist sandy soil until rooted. The plants will last for several years and they should be pruned back each year to maintain

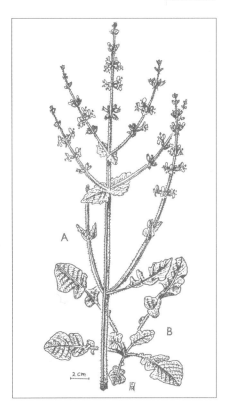

Fig. 26. Judaean sage *Salvia judaica*, with a rosette of leaves.

compact growth. A very decorative sage native in the Holy Land is the annual horminum clary, *S. horminum*, with purple, pink or white terminal bracts. It is like the French lavender *Lavandula stoechas*, also found there, a splendid fragrant undershrub which should be included in any biblical garden.

Species

Salvia judaica, Israel, the authentic species, annual (see fig. 26)

S. horminum (also known as *S. viridis*), horminum clary, Mediterranean region, annual 30cm (1ft); sow in spring, where required to flower, in a sunny spot (see pl. 45).

S. officinalis, perennial culinary sage, S. Europe, the cultivar 'Purpureus' has dark purple leaves

S. pratensis, field clary, Europe and Morocco, perennial, purple flowers, favours chalk and limestone

Pl. 45. Horminum clary, decorative sage *Salvia horminum*.

Tulip (*Tulipa*)

The scarlet mountain tulip (*Tulipa montana*) flowers in semi-desert areas of the Holy Land during early spring: 'The flowers appear on the earth; the time of singing has come, and the voice of the turtle-dove is heard in our land' (Song of Solomon 2:12). It may also be one of the biblical 'lilies' (see p.30). Red tulips are well known in cultivation, with several Middle Eastern species and their hybrids being favourite bulbs in rock gardens, unlike the taller varieties which are regimented as bedding plants. Although the mountain tulip itself may be impossible to obtain from commercial sources, one of the others listed below would be an admirable substitute as they have scarlet flowers, sometimes with black and yellow at the base inside. The grey-green leaves are often attractively crinkled along their margins.

Cultivation

Be sure to plant the bulbs in autumn in a sunny situation with well-drained soil, or they will rot away. In fact, it may be better to lift them in summer, when the leaves have withered, and store them in a warm garden shed or wherever they will be thoroughly ripened. They can also be grown in pots and re-potted each year. Propagation is either by off-set bulbs (which do not always occur) or by seeds which take several years to develop into bulbs of flowering size. One of the advantages of these species tulips in cultivation is that they flower earlier than the hybrids and contrast with the daffodils and other yellow flowers at that season.

Species

Tulipa eichleri, Iran, 30cm (12in.) high, flowers large, does well in a warm spot and need not be lifted each season

Pl. 46. Cultivated Asian Tulip *Tulipa fosteriana*.

T. fosteriana, southern Russia, 20-45cm (8-18in.) high, often hybridised with other species producing orange or yellow streaked flowers instead of the typical scarlet ones (see pl. 46)

T. greigii, southern Russia, 20-25cm (8-10in.) high, flowers large, often

scarlet though sometimes orange or yellow

T. montana (including *T. sharonensis*), Israel, 20cm (8in.) high, bulb tunic woolly inside, not usually available commercially but it may be a parent of scarlet garden hybrids (see fig. 27)

Fig. 27. Tulip *Tulipa montana*.

3
Shrubs and Small Trees

Woody-stemmed plants – shrubs and trees – do not die down like herbaceous plants. Even if they lose their leaves, as deciduous trees do, new buds develop the following season; while evergreens keep their leaves throughout the year.

Some shrubs are very small and low-growing, while others are larger and difficult to distinguish from small trees. I have divided them by a basic feature, the stem: shrubs having several stems and trees only a single one. Stragglers such as the rose and the climbing vine are also included in this section.

Shrubs and trees provide continuity in a garden and by careful siting they can be enjoyed at all times of the year. However, consider their requirements before planting or they will not develop fully or may even die. Some need open positions while others tolerate shade; some need moisture throughout the year while others thrive on dry banks; some are hardy while others need protection.

Planting
Prepare the ground well, incorporating rotten manure and bonemeal into the soil at the bottom of the hole in which the shrub or tree is to be planted. Make sure that the hole is larger than the roots or they will be crowded together and unable to grow properly, especially in the critical first year, when establishment is important. Replace

Pl. 47. White broom, *Retama raetam*.

the soil over the roots and tread in firmly so that the plant does not sway in the wind and work loose. Water in, and do not let the roots dry up while they are becoming established. Nowadays container-grown plants may be planted all year round, but this apart, deciduous ones should be planted during their dormant season, and

evergreens at the beginning of their growth in order not to interrupt it.

Pruning
Pruning is often badly done because the simple principles are unknown or ignored. I cannot deal fully with the subject here: many gardening books cover it well, species by species. But generally speak-

ing, pruning of shrubs is necessary to reduce their overall size or to encourage flower and fruit production. If the latter, as in vines, the previous season's growth is cut away in order to channel nourishment into a few flowering buds.

Frequently unsightly lopping of trees is taken for pruning. Pruning properly done should leave the tree looking well-balanced in appearance, without abrupt truncations or 'snag ends' – the short lengths of branches that are often left by pruners who neglect to cut them back flush with the trunk. If you prune cleanly, flush with the trunk, the wound heals and is covered by new bark. Snag ends, on the contrary, either sprout furiously with a mass of little twigs or, more usually, die, become rotten and infect the trunk itself, from which it may never recover. A smaller, shapely tree is often best obtained by thinning out complete branches.

Deciduous shrubs and small trees should be pruned with sharp secateurs, mainly during their dormant season. Always cut just above the bud which is to continue the growth of the shoot. Evergreens, if they need to be pruned at all, are best done during their growing season.

Pl. 48. Box tree *Buxus sempervirens*.

Pl. 49. Laurustinus *Viburnum tinus*.

Box Tree (*Buxus*); Laurustinus (*Viburnum*)

In the Authorised (King James) Version, the 'box tree' or 'box' is mentioned – 'I will set in the desert the fir tree, and the pine, and the box tree together' (Isaiah 41:19), and, 'The glory of Lebanon shall come unto thee, the fir tree, the pine tree, and the box together' (Isaiah 60:13), though the New Revised Standard Version has the plane tree in place of the box, and Professor Michael Zohary considers the laurustinus bush to be the species concerned (its Arabic name is similar to the Hebrew word used in the Bible). So if you have space in your biblical garden why not grow all three!

The box is better known as a bush in a tub or as a trimmed hedge than as a free-growing tree. Its small, evergreen leaves are neat and grow close together, making it an ideal plant for clipping. In early spring its tiny yellow flowers are inconspicuous but beautifully fragrant. The tree grows very slowly and lives for centuries, hence its wood is dense and used for carving and wood-cut printing.

Laurustinus is also an evergreen, but with much larger, thinner leaves than the box and flat heads of white, pink-tinged flowers right through the winter, making it a valuable addition to your all-year-round garden as a background screen.

For the plane tree, see page 68.

Cultivation

Box: plant in spring as a background bush in the open or in partial shade. Before planting dig out the soil and work in well-rotted manure. Trim annually in spring or late summer, not

Fig. 28. Box tree *Buxus sempervirens*, with male and female flowers.

in winter. Hard frosts can turn some leaves brown, so it may be worthwhile to cover bushes in cold regions with sacks or cloths or plastic sheets. It can be propagated from rooted divisions or by cuttings of young shoots inserted in a moist shady place in late summer.

Laurustinus: plant in partial shade in autumn or spring, in ordinary light soil. Cuttings inserted under a jam jar during the summer root fairly readily, as do layered roots taken in autumn and left for a year. In winter thin out weak stems, otherwise avoid pruning.

Species

Buxus sempervirens, W. and S. Europe and W. Asia, including Lebanon; tree grows up to 4m (13ft) high, but is usually clipped; for edgings and small bushes use cultivar 'Suffruticosa', the dwarf box, which is slow-growing (see fig. 28 and pl. 48)

Viburnum tinus, Mediterranean region, including Israel; grows up to 3m (10ft), but usually much less, and spreading sideways; severe frost may kill plants in cold countries (see pl. 49)

Pl. 50. Judas tree *Cercis siliquastrum*.

Judas Tree (*Cercis*)

It was Judas Iscariot, one of Jesus' twelve disciples, who betrayed his master to be crucified; and when he realised what he had done, gave the blood money back to the priests, saying, 'I have sinned by betraying innocent blood.' 'Throwing down the pieces of silver in the temple, he departed; and he went and hanged himself' (Matthew 27:4,5). We have no means of telling what tree he chose, but traditionally *Cercis siliquastrum*, now known as the Judas tree, has been said to be the one. This is because it bears its numerous, purple-red, pea flowers along its branches in spring before the new leaves develop, so the tradition grew up that these were the drops of blood of Judas. Although strictly this is not a biblical plant it is a highly desirable small garden tree.

Cultivation

The Judas tree is easily grown from seed: those I have raised flowered when eight or nine years old. Severe frosts may cut back seedlings and young growth, but otherwise it is hardy, favouring a sunny position where it can develop as a shrub or pos-

sibly a small tree. Avoid transplanting and root disturbance.

Species

Cercis siliquastrum, Judas tree, tree of Judea, Holy Land and E. Mediterranean (see fig. 29 and pl. 50)

C. canadensis, redbud, N. America, remarkably similar to, and a very suitable substitute for, the Old World species, especially in cold areas

Fig. 29. Judas tree *Cercis siliquastrum* in fruit with flowers.

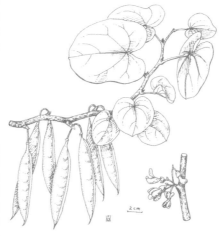

Rock-rose, Ladanum (*Cistus*)

True myrrh is a resin obtained from a tropical African bush (see p. 84) so it is unlikely that the Ishmaelite traders, referred to in Genesis 37:25 – 'coming from Gilead, with their camels carrying gum, balm, and resin [KJV, RSV myrrh]' – travelling southwards along the ancient road to Egypt, would have been carrying a tropical product. Local products, including 'myrrh', were also sent down to Egypt by Jacob (Genesis 43:11). It is generally considered that the 'myrrh' in each case is the ladanum resin obtained from rock-roses (*Cistus* species) which grow abundantly on hot, limestone hillsides in the Mediterranean region. They are evergreen bushes with large, rose-like flowers having five crinkled, white or pink petals. Only certain species yield the resin which makes the leaves, stems and sepals sticky and shiny, at least during the summer. The yellowish resin is used medicinally and in perfumery, including incense-burning. Incidentally, the 'gum' the Ishmaelite traders carried was gum tragacanth obtained from *Astragalus gummifer*, p. 31; for 'balm' see pp. 45, 48, 49, 88.

Pl. 51. Rock-rose *Cistus creticus*.

Cultivation

Some rock-roses are reasonably hardy but all need a sunny position where they can ripen in summer. A hard winter, however, will either kill or severely cut back many species so it is advisable to choose a sheltered position in cold districts and protect in winter. Well-drained ordinary soil is suitable and they thrive in alkaline conditions. Bought plants should be planted out during the growing season after the threat of frost has passed. Seedlings can be raised by sowing the tiny seeds on sandy soil in a frame in spring and transplanting the seedlings outside in early summer. They should flower during the second year. Cuttings taken in late summer root easily but need protection during the winter. Many species are in cultivation; the ones listed below are actually resinous.

Species

Cistus creticus (also known as C. *incanus*, and C. *villosus* var. *creticus*), E. Mediterranean, 1m (3ft), hairy leaves, resinous in summer, flowers pink (see pl. 51)

Fig. 30. Rock-rose *Cistus laurifolius*.

C. *x cyprius*, a commonly cultivated hybrid with white flowers that may or may not have dark petal spots

C. *ladanifer*, generally regarded as the ladanum bush but not the one of the Bible as it occurs in Spain, flowers white with dark spot at the base of each petal

C. *laurifolius*, Turkey, 2-2.5m (6-8ft), whole plant resinous, flowers white; the biblical ladanum (see fig. 30 and pl. 53)

Fig Tree (*Ficus*)

Most of us are familiar with fig fruits in the dried state and in confectionery; fresh figs soon deteriorate in shops. In biblical times dried figs were an important item of food (1 Samuel 25:18; 1 Chronicles 12:40) to tide over the lean winter months, but fresh figs were especially favoured as the first fruits of summer (Hosea 9:10; Amos 8:1-2). Fig trees grown beside houses offered welcome shade for sitting (Zechariah 3:10, John 1:48), while Jesus used the fig tree in his parables (Matthew 7:16, Luke 13:6ff; 21:29-30) and on one occasion he cursed a fig tree which withered and died (Mark 11:13, 20).

When the common fig (*Ficus carica*) is grown in open ground in warm countries it develops as a small tree with a spreading crown of thick branches and twigs. But when planted against a wall it often has several trunks and is continually cut back only to sprout side shoots. Such shoots grow quickly, 1m (3ft) or more a year, with large lobed leaves which develop late in spring; although rough to the touch, they were sewn together by Adam and Eve to form aprons (Genesis 3:7). Two crops of fruit develop: one in early summer from the previous year's growth, and the second on

Pl. 53. Rock-rose *Cistus laurifolius*.

Pl. 52. Common fig tree *Ficus carica*, north of Jerusalem.

Pl. 54. Sycomore fig tree *Ficus sycomorus*.

Pl. 55. Young fig leaves and fruits.

...he new shoots. Botanically the fig fruits are interesting as they are composed of numerous minute flowers which line the inner cavity; pollination of wild figs is by wasps but the cultivated figs are self-fertilised.

Another species of fig is the sycomore (*Ficus sycomorus*) referred to several times in the Old Testament (e.g. 1 Kings 10:27; Amos 7:14) and in the New Testament as the tree up which Zacchaeus climbed to see Jesus (Luke 19:4). As it is a subtropical species it could be included in Bible gardens in warm countries if there is space.

Cultivation

Cuttings of 2-3 year-old twigs of the common fig usually root very easily in pots and grow well in ordinary soil mixed with lime rubble. If planted too close to a wall the rapidly expanding trunk could cause damage. Beware also of the extensive roots which take nourishment from the surrounding soil; by planting in a sunken tub the roots will be restricted. In dry weather water well and during a very severe winter frost protect the branches with mats or polythene sheets; in cold climates plants grown in tubs need to be wintered inside.

Twigs of the sycomore fig will also root as cuttings, provided they are not too moist and are kept warm. They will develop into trees with fruits on the branches and trunks. In due time they form huge trees.

Note that nowadays the name 'sycamore' is applied to *Acer* (UK) and *Platanus* (USA).

Species

Ficus carica (including *F. palmata*, the wild form), common fig, Syria to Afghanistan; several named varieties are available, of which the best for gardens in Britain and elsewhere with similar climates is 'Brown Turkey' (see pls 52 and 55)

F. sycomorus, sycomore, sycomore fig, tropical Africa extending to Israel, suitable for warm countries (see fig. 31a and pl. 54)

Fig. 31a Sycomore fig *Ficus sycomorus*.

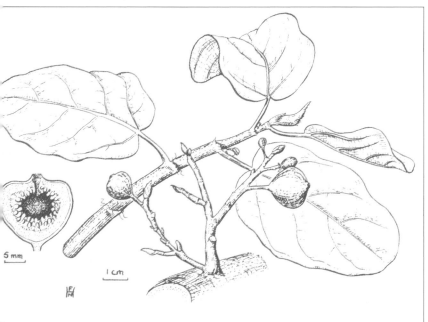

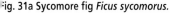

Bay Tree (*Laurus*)

The bay tree, also known as the sweet bay, is the true laurel of ancient times which was used to decorate athletes and even the Roman emperor. Hence St Paul refers to the athlete in training: 'They do it to receive a perishable garland' (1 Corinthians 9:25) in comparison with a Christian whose crown will last for ever. The bay may also be the green tree referred to in Psalm 37:35.

In the Mediterranean region the bay occurs on rocky hillsides, such as Mount Carmel. Old specimens grow into trees up to 12m (40ft) high, but usually much less, with numerous branches and leafy shoots. The leathery bay leaves are well known in the dry state as a condiment in cooking. The male and female flowers are borne on separate trees in spring: they are yellow but unspectacular. The fruits are like black olives in autumn. It is an evergreen growing quite slowly in cultivation so it is often seen as a shrub in tubs or as a hedge pruned into shape in spring.

Pl. 57. Bay tree *Laurus nobilis*.

Cultivation

Although quite hardy in western Europe, the roots of young plants in containers should not be frozen, nor should they dry out in summer. Propagation is easy but slow, from short, leafy shoots inserted into sandy leafmould or peat, during late summer. Plant in spring in ordinary soil in a position where it will become a green background to smaller colourful plants. In cold climates plants in tubs will need to be wintered inside a greenhouse.

Species

Laurus nobilis, bay tree, sweet bay, laurel, Mediterranean region (see fig. 31 and pl. 57)

Storax Tree (*Liquidambar, Styrax*)

The resin 'stacte', an ingredient of the holy anointing oil (Exodus 30:34), is probably the same as the 'balm' which the Ishmaelite traders were carrying to Egypt when Joseph was sold to them by his brothers (Genesis 37:25). Later,

Pl. 58. Levant storax *Styrax officinalis*.

Fig. 31. Bay tree *Laurus nobilis*, flowering and fruiting shoots.

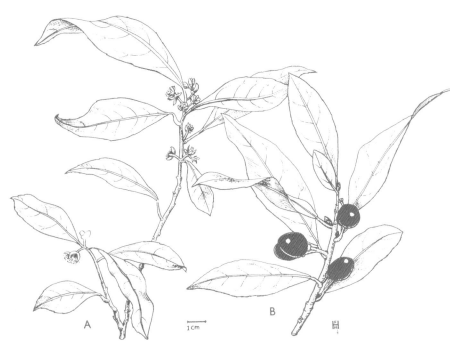

Pl. 59. Levant storax *Styrax officinalis*.

Fig. 32. Storax *Liquidambar orientalis* in flower and fruit.

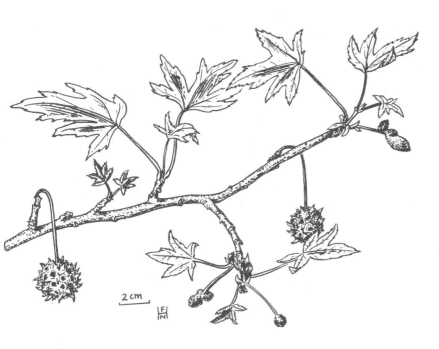

his brothers took 'a little balm' as a present to Joseph from his father, Israel (Genesis 43:11). This is most likely to have been the resin yielded by the storax tree (*Liquidambar orientalis*) or lentisc bush (*Pistacia lentiscus*, see p. 88), but there is a tradition that the other storax tree (*Styrax officinalis*) at one time also produced resin which it no longer yields. The latter is also said to be the 'poplar' that was peeled by Jacob (Genesis 30:37) (see poplar, p. 69).

The *Liquidambar* is a small tree with digitately lobed leaves that turn yellow before falling in autumn. The small yellowish flowers are clustered in round pendant heads. It belongs to the witch-hazel family, *Hamamelidaceae*.

The *Styrax* is a bush or small deciduous tree, profusely branched and with rounded leaves attractively silvery white on the undersurface. Numerous white flowers hang all over the plant among the leaves in spring or early summer. It belongs to its own family, *Styracaceae*.

Cultivation

Liquidambar can be grown from seeds, which may take two years to germinate, and a really warm moist site is best. *Styrax* needs a sunny position, against a wall in cold areas, where the leaves and flowers can be seen at close quarters. Plant during winter months in well-drained peaty soil. Propagate by layering shoots.

Species

Liquidambar orientalis, storax, Asia Minor, the biblical species (see fig. 32)

L. styraciflua, sweet gum, USA, a substitute for the above, forming a taller tree, 30m (100ft) or more, with spectacular red autumn colour

Styrax officinalis, Levant storax, Mediterranean region (see pls 58 and 59)

S. japonica, Japan, very similar to the last and could be used as a substitute

Thorns, Brambles (*Lycium, Rubus*)

Since so many dry-country plants are prickly or thorny it is not surprising that they are often mentioned in the Scriptures. Our problem is to know which ones to include in a biblical garden – we have already mentioned the prickly thistles (p. 24) and here we deal with some thorny shrubs (Numbers 33:55; Judges 9:14; Proverbs 22:5; Luke 6:44).

The boxthorn (*Lycium europaeum*) forms a deciduous thorny bush about 2m (6ft) high and as much across. Its small tubular purple flowers in summer are followed by round orange berries which are edible and favoured by birds. Seeds or hard wood cuttings grow easily in well-drained soil and most species of *Lycium* may be used as a hedge in open situations.

Brambles or blackberries (*Rubus* species) are all rather similar although there are dozens of confusing species. They grow easily from seeds and form a tangle in hedgerows or thickets with very prickly stems which can become a pest in a garden if unchecked. In late summer the black fruits are best stewed or preserved as jelly.

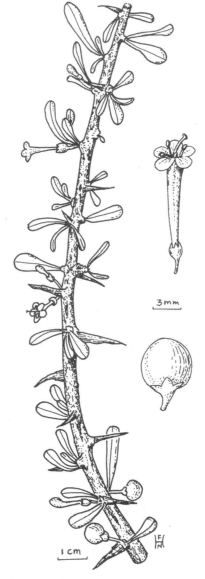

Fig. 33. Boxthorn *Lycium europaeum*, with a flower and a fruit.

Species

Lycium europaeum, boxthorn, Mediterranean region; withstands wind and salt spray, but tender. The hardy, trailing *L. chinense*, tea-tree, is a poor substitute since it is not thorny! (See fig. 33)

Rubus sanguineus (formerly *R. sanctus*), holy bramble, E. Mediterranean region; a plant is guarded at St Catherine's Monastery, Sinai, as the 'burning bush' (Exodus 3:2-6) (see pl. 60)

R. fruticosus, blackberry, Europe and elsewhere, similar to the holy bramble and could be used as a substitute

R. laciniatus, cut-leaved blackberry, USA, the cultivated species which is more controllable than the European one

Apple (*Malus*) and Apricot (*Prunus*)

There has been a great deal of discussion as to whether the apple or the apricot is the fruit mentioned in two

Fig. 34. Apricot *Prunus armeniaca*, with flowers and a cut-open fruit.

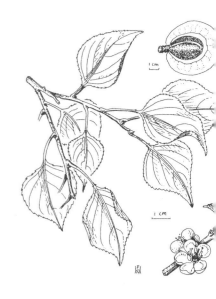

Pl. 60. Holy bramble *Rubus sanguineus* (right) beside a stream on Carmel.

Pl. 61. Apricot *Prunus armeniaca*.

against a wall. It tolerates lighter chalky soils than the apple which needs good loam and plenty of manure or compost over the roots each year. According to the space available, it is possible to grow them as bushes, standards, cordons or full trees. Pruning in winter should limit long growth and encourage the formation of flower buds on the short shoots. Plant and transplant only during winter, unless container-grown plants are obtained.

Species

Malus domestica (also called *Pyrus malus*), apple, Europe. There are many cultivated varieties and you should choose one that does well in your area and bears fruits you like; flowering late spring, pale pink, fruits ripen late summer (see pl. 62)

Prunus armeniaca, apricot, China, flowering early spring, white or pale pink, fruits mature in summer, orange coloured with a large stone (see fig. 34 and pl. 61)

biblical passages: 'Sustain me with raisins, refresh me with apples; for I am faint with love' (Song of Solomon 2:5); and, 'The vine withers, the fig tree droops. Pomegranate, palm, and apple – all the trees of the field are dried up; surely, joy withers away among the people' (Joel 1:12). At one time it was thought that apples would not grow successfully in the Holy Land, but that is not so. Neither tree is native to the

Holy Land. Both would have had to be introduced from countries to the north and east.

Cultivation

Both are small trees and very suitable for a garden. In cooler countries the apricot does better when grown

Pl. 62. Apple *Malus 'James Grieve'*.

Mulberry (*Morus*)

Most authorities agree that Luke 17:6 refers to the *black* mulberry: 'The apostles said to the Lord, "Increase our faith!" The Lord replied, "If you had faith the size of a mustard seed, you could say to this mulberry [RSV sycamine] tree, 'Be uprooted and planted in the sea', and it would obey you."'

The black mulberry is a medium-sized deciduous tree that eventually develops a stout knobbly trunk. Its leaves sprout quite late in the spring; they are heart-shaped, stiff and rough to the touch. Male catkins and female

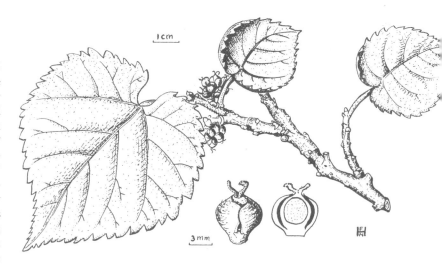

Fig. 35. Black mulberry *Morus nigra*, with two mature flowers, one cut open.

Pl. 63. Black mulberry *Morus nigra*.

flower clusters appear before the leaves come. The fruits are composed of a number of female flowers coalescing and maturing to a juicy, dark red berry, like a loganberry (but with a different structure), best eaten as jam or made into wine.

The *white* mulberry is the food of silkworms in China, and although the moth caterpillars will eat black mulberry leaves they are said to produce an inferior silk. Silk, referred to in Revelation 18:12, would then have been imported from China along the 'silk route' through Iran.

Pl. 64. Black mulberry *Morus nigra* flower.

Cultivation

The black mulberry is hardy enough to be planted in an open sunny position except in cooler latitudes where it should be protected by a wall. Water frequently after planting. It grows quickly but may take some fifteen years to fruit. Old trees benefit by having stones and soil thrown against the base of the trunk to anchor the roots and enable suckers to become established. In this way some English trees have persisted since the time of James I – the King James to whom the Authorised Version was dedicated in 1611. Regular mulching with old manure in the autumn can be followed in early spring with a light dressing of nitrate of soda and potash. Propagation is possible from seeds sown in warm conditions, or by half-ripened cuttings taken from the upper part of the tree in late summer.

Species

Morus alba, white mulberry, China, a larger-sized tree with a more open growth than the black mulberry, and bearing white or pink fruits turning dark red

M. nigra, black mulberry, Caspian Sea region and long grown in the Mediterranean region (see fig. 35 and pls 63 and 64)

Myrtle (*Myrtus*)

This lovely evergreen bush grows on the hillsides in the Holy Land and it was one of those leafy plants used by the Jews for making booths (or tabernacles) at the Feast of Tabernacles, as a reminder of their exodus from Egypt (Leviticus 23:40-43; Nehemiah 8:15). The prophet Isaiah envisaged myrtle as one day replacing the prickly brier of the desert (Isaiah 41:19; 55:13). Even Esther's name, *Hadassah*, was derived from the Hebrew word for myrtle (Esther 2:7).

Its glossy leaves are very fragrant as they contain oil in minute glands

Pl. 65. Common myrtle *Myrtus communis*.

which can be seen through a hand lens when a leaf is held up to the light. Its flowers are also fragrant. They appear in summer all over the branches as white stars, each flower having five petal lobes and a mass of stamens. Its fruits are black, like an olive, and are said to be edible.

Fig 36. Myrtle *Myrtus communis*.

Cultivation

Myrtle can be grown successfully in milder areas such as southern England, though it may be frosted brown or even killed during very hard winters unless protected by a wall. Elsewhere it is advisable to grow myrtle in a tub which can be overwintered inside. Propagation is easily achieved by cuttings from half-ripened shoots in summer, or by layering lower branches which can be weighted down with a rock for several months. Myrtle will tolerate both moist and dry soil and it does well on limestone and chalk. Bushes in full sun flower better than those in shady positions. Pruning is only necessary to maintain a compact bush or to prevent encroachment and is best done in spring or summer.

Species

Myrtus communis, common myrtle, Mediterranean region, 1-2m (3-6ft) high; the cultivar 'Tarentina' is compacter and it has numerous much smaller leaves and whitish fruits; cv 'Leucocarpa' also has white fruits; and cv 'Variegata' has white and green leaves, but it is rather tender (see fig. 36 and pl. 65)

Olive (*Olea*)

The olive tree is to be seen throughout the Mediterranean region where it is extensively cultivated. In the Holy Land the rounded, grey-green trees occur in groves on the rocky, terraced hillsides, where they have long been grown as important fruit trees, yielding not only their edible black fruits, but also olive oil for cooking and ointments. The oil is extracted by crushing the fruits in autumn and pressing the pulp with a millstone in a press. Oil presses were located among the trees and sometimes gave rise to the name of the place, such as the Mount of Olives (Mark 14:26) and the Garden of Gethsemane, which in Hebrew means 'the garden of the oil press' (Matthew 26:36). The oil was also used for anointing the king (1 Samuel 10:1); the Messiah (Christ) is the anointed one of God. Olive trees are evergreen and very long-lived, old trees having gnarled hollow trunks. The leaves are narrow and willow-like; the small flowers have four petals and only two stamens.

Pl. 66. Olive tree *Olea europaea* in the Garden of Gethsemane, Jerusalem.

Cultivation

The olive requires a Mediterranean kind of climate to thrive, that is, a cool moist winter and hot dry summer. It will grow elsewhere, such as southern England, preferably in the protection of a wall, but may be shrubby and will seldom fruit unless the summer is hot. However, it is well worth growing, either outside or in a cool greenhouse, as it is such an important biblical species. Plants can be raised from seeds but the spiny, small-leaved wild form, the oleaster mentioned by St Paul (Romans 11:17), may result, whereas propagation by cuttings is certain to yield the true cultivated olive. Protect young plants by bringing them inside or by surrounding them with brushwood in severe winter weather. If the leaves are frosted, new shoots should break from older wood.

Species

Olea europaea, cultivated olive, Middle East (see fig. 37 and pls 66 and 67); and the wild olive, var. *sylvestris* (or *oleaster*)

Pl. 67. Green olive fruits.

Fig. 37. Olive *Olea europaea* with a flower and two fruits, one cut open.

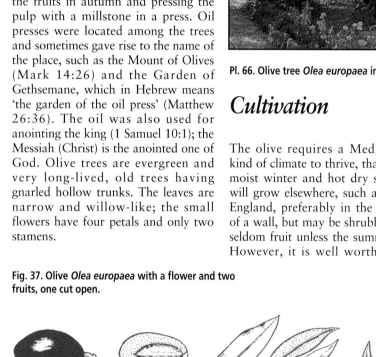

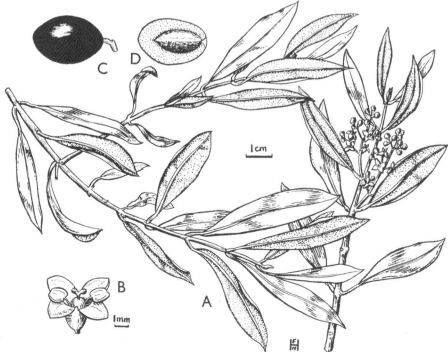

Pl. 68. Almond *Prunus dulcis.*

Fig. 38. Almond *Prunus dulcis*, with flowers, a cleaned fruit and a seed.

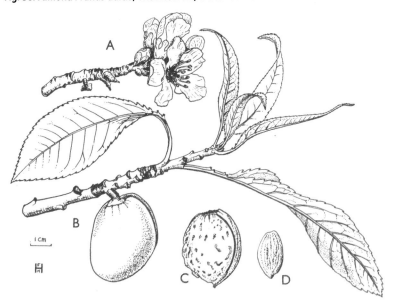

Almond Tree
(*Prunus*)

Almond nuts were carried to Egypt by Joseph's brothers (Genesis 43:11); twigs of almond budded and fruited overnight to prove that Aaron was God's man to assist Moses (Numbers 17:8) and the holy lampstand had cups shaped like almond flowers (Exodus 25:33; 37:19).

This is a delightful small deciduous tree suitable for most gardens. It flowers very early in the year before the leaves appear and the numerous large white flowers are tinged pink. The young velvety fruits are often eaten whole in the Middle East but the majority are left to mature for the nuts. The delicious kernel, the sweet or Jordan almond, is obtained by cracking open the hard casing. However, the ornamental almond with pink flowers often grown in Britain has bitter nuts which should be eaten in limited quantities as they contain a minute amount of prussic acid.

Cultivation

It is easily grown in a sunny position, preferably on light soil and the flowers are best seen against a dark background early in the year. A mature almond tree spreads sideways with lots of branchlets, so enough space should be available for it to develop.

Species

Prunus dulcis (formerly *P. amydalus*, and *Amygdalus communis*), S.E. Europe and S.W. Asia, 6-9m (20-30ft), many cultivars of the sweet almond may be grown for the nuts in warmer countries, while the ornamental cultivars succeed in cooler climates (see fig. 38 and pls 47 and 68)

55

Pomegranate (*Punica*)

One of the characteristic shrubs of the Mediterranean region is the pomegranate. It is well known for its round fruits which are about the size of an orange but have a very different structure inside. The numerous seeds are enclosed in a pale, watery pulp which is very refreshing to eat in hot weather. The fruit is surmounted by the persistent calyx and it is said that this inspired the form of royal crowns. The bright scarlet flowers that precede the fruits are very attractive throughout the summer and make the pomegranate well worthwhile cultivating even if the climatic conditions do not permit the setting of fruit. The pomegranate plant is deciduous, with oval leathery leaves not developing until early summer, and though it is usually a densely branched bush it can become a small tree, up to 10m (33ft) high in favourable areas.

No wonder that such an attractive and useful plant is frequently mentioned in the Bible. The bell-shaped flowers and the round fruits modelled

Pl. 69. Pomegranate shrub *Punica granatum* 'Nana'.

in gold hemmed the priests' long robes – 'Pomegranates of blue and purple and scarlet stuff . . . with bells of gold between them' (Exodus 28:33-34). The pomegranate was one of the fruits of the Promised Land (Deuteronomy 8:8) and its Hebrew name, *rimmon*, was applied to locations (Numbers 33:19-20) and people (2 Samuel 4:2).

Cultivation

A warm situation in full sun is required and the added protection of a sun-facing wall in cold localities; elsewhere a cool greenhouse is necessary. If outside plants are frosted they usually sprout from lower buds, but it is as well to overwinter cuttings inside to replace any killed. Any good soil will do, providing it is light and well drained. Propagation is by cuttings or layers taken in summer; plants raised from seeds are unlikely to be of good quality.

Species

Punica granatum, native of S.E. Europe and the Middle East, now widely cultivated (see fig. 39, fruit); typically the flowers have 5-7 scarlet petals and numerous yellowish stamens, but there are other cultivars: 'Flore-pleno', numerous red petals; 'Legrellii', double flowers with petals striped red and whitish; 'Albescens', whitish flowers; cv 'Nana' is recommended for small gardens as it is hardier and dwarf, seldom being more than 30cm (1ft) high, yet with miniature scarlet flowers like the typical pomegranate (see pl. 69)

Fig. 39. Pomegranate *Punica granatum*, whole and cut fruit.

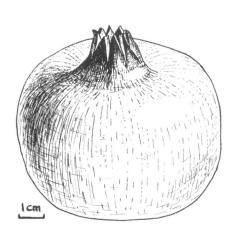

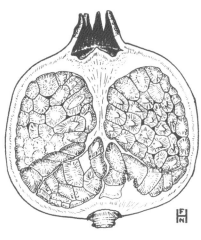

Broom (*Retama*)

The dramatic story of the prophet Elijah fleeing from Queen Jezebel who wanted to take his life, includes an account of how Elijah rested under a broom tree (1 Kings 19:4, 'juniper' of KJV). He fled to the desert where one of the few plants that could offer shade is the white broom (*Retama raetam*). Even that is more of a shrub than a tree and its mass of thin, almost leafless branches would not provide deep shade, but it was better than nothing. When in full bloom the myriads of white pea flowers are a splendid sight. Its roots make good charcoal which was sometimes attached to incendiary arrows (Psalm 120:4).

Pl. 70. Spanish broom *Spartium junceum* at Ephesus.

Cultivation

The white broom is a tender plant that will not stand much frost, although I have had plants in flower in London. Its seeds may be difficult to obtain for your Bible garden. A very suitable substitute is one of the white *Cytisus* species listed below, or even the beautifully fragrant, yellow-flowered Spanish broom, which is actually a feature of hillside thickets in the Holy Land and elsewhere in the Mediterranean region. They are all easily grown from seeds and need a sunny position with light soil. Plant in their permanent position while young.

Fig. 40. White broom *Retama raetam* of the Holy Land, with flowers, pod and seed.

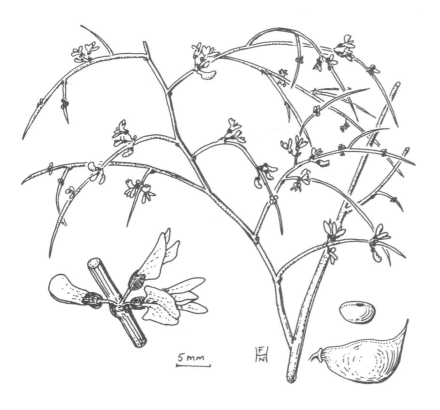

5 mm

Species

Cytisus multiflorus (also called *C. albus*), white broom, Spain, 3m (10ft), hardy

C. x praecox, a commonly cultivated hybrid with a dense growth, 1-2m (3-6ft) high, and yellow-white flowers, hardy

Retama raetam, white broom, E. Mediterranean, the correct species, 3m (10ft), tender (see fig. 40)

Spartium junceum, Spanish broom, Mediterranean region, 2-3m (6-10ft), mid to late summer, yellow flowers, fairly hardy (see pl. 70)

Rose (*Rosa*)

Nobody is sure whether the true rose is mentioned in the Bible although most translations include the name (for instance, 'I am a rose of Sharon', Song of Solomon 2:1) for plants where it is more likely that crocus, narcissus or tulip was meant. But both the dog-rose and the Phoenician rose grow in the Holy Land and it would be a pity to exclude all roses from your Bible garden. Even if the white Phoenician rose is impossible to obtain, a bush of the wild dog-rose with its pale pink single flowers and red hips would be a delightful addition, but remember that it is prickly.

Pl. 71. Dog-rose *Rosa canina.*

Fig. 41. Phoenician rose *Rosa phoenicia.*

Cultivation

Best grown in a hedge or up a pergola where the straggly shoots can be tied back. The wild plants will not need as much attention and manuring as popular garden roses. Prune old growths after flowering, in summer, if necessary.

Species

Rosa canina, dog-rose, Europe to C. and S.W. Asia, 2m (6ft), hardy, flowers early in summer; there are many similar wild species with single flowers (see pl. 71)

R. x damascena, Damask rose, hybrid between *R. phoenicia* and *R. gallica*, early summer flowering semi-double pink, cv 'Trigintipetala' is the source of fragrant rose-water and attar of roses

R. phoenicia, Phoenician rose, W. Asia, tender (see fig. 41)

Tamarisk (*Tamarix*)

Abraham planted a tamarisk tree in Beersheba (Genesis 21:33), and Saul was sitting under one, spear in hand, when he heard news of David's rebellion against him (1 Samuel 22:6). Later, when Saul and his three sons fell in battle, the triumphant Philistines hung their bodies from the wall of Beth Shan, but Saul's men rescued them and buried the bones honourably under a tamarisk tree (1 Samuel 31:13).

Some species grow in the desert, others along water courses. They have a heath-like appearance and are often no more than shrubs or small trees with elongated heads of tiny white or pink flowers. The twigs are leafless or bear minute scale leaves.

Cultivation

Tamarisks are often planted near the coast as they withstand salty winds and many species are hardy and do well on light soil anywhere. Hard-prune after a few years to avoid a straggly appearance. Allow plenty of room for their far-reaching roots. Propagation is by pencil-sized cuttings in late summer in sandy soil.

Fig. 42. Tamarisk *Tamarix ramosissima*, with scale-leaves and a flower.

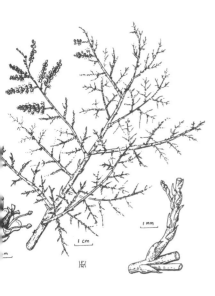

Pl. 72. Tamarisk *Tamarix ramosissima*.

Species

Tamarisk aphylla, S.W. Asia and N. Africa, one of the biblical species, tender large tree of the desert

T. gallica, Europe, evergreen, flowers white and pink late summer

T. ramosissima (usually known as *T. pentandra*) S.E. Europe and W. Asia, deciduous, flowers pink midsummer (see fig. 42 and pl. 72)

T. tetrandra S.E. Europe and W. Asia, deciduous shrub, flowers pink before leaves in spring.

Grapevine (*Vitis*)

The grapevine is one of the most important fruits of the Holy Land, so it is not surprising that it is frequently mentioned in the Bible. The first reference to it is that unfortunate occurrence when Noah became drunk with wine (Genesis 9:21), but many happier incidents are included both in the Old and New Testaments. Wine gladdens the human heart (Psalm 104:15), it is also a mocker (Proverbs 20:1), and yet was used at symbolic occasions such as the Passover and Last Supper (Matthew 26:27-29; 1 Corinthians 11:25). Raisins rejoiced David's men (1 Chronicles 12:40). Israel was likened to a vineyard (Isaiah 5:1-10); and Jesus said, 'I am the true vine' (John 15:1).

The vine is a climbing shrub that

may be grown on walls or arbours near houses to give shade, or commercially in vineyards which are often on sunny hillsides where drainage is good. The long growths are cut back severely during winter in order to concentrate the nourishment into a few buds. In spring as the leafless branch sprouts from the dormant buds, large five-lobed leaves develop alternately on the new shoot with a tendril opposite each leaf. At about the fifth and sixth leaf instead of a tendril a flower truss appears which ultimately develops into a bunch of green or black grapes. Grapes are eaten as fresh fruit, dried as raisins (also currants and sultanas), or pressed into wine. Young vine leaves are cooked with rice, as an envelope.

Pl. 73. Grapevine *Vitis vinifera* in fruit.

Cultivation

Container-grown plants can be planted at any time of the year but preferably in winter. Prepare the bed well with good drainage and deeply dug-in old manure. A suitable position in a Bible garden is against a wall or fence, or where the branches can be trained over an archway or pergola as a decorative feature even if climatic conditions do not allow grapes to ripen outside. In such areas an unheated greenhouse could be used but this may detach it from the context of the biblical garden.

Fig. 43. Vine *Vitis vinifera* in flower.

Adequate watering and ventilation are required to prevent mildew forming on leaves and fruits; sulphur or copper sprays kill mildew. Mulching and feeding with a balanced fertiliser produces good fruits. The method of training and pruning your vine depends on the space available but it is essential to hard-prune lateral shoots back to the main stems each winter. Propagation is easy by taking green cuttings having two or three buds and inserting them in soil in a warm place, or from hardwood cuttings in winter and rooted outside. Plants raised from seeds from fresh grapes or those sprouting in compost are likely to be disappointing. Full details of cultivation and pruning are provided in many publications, such as the *Wisley Handbook*.

Species

Vitis vinifera, known only in cultivation, though probably developed from *V. sylvestris* wild in the Caspian region (see fig. 43 and pls 6 and 73). A few of the many cultivars are listed here (specialist advice should be sought about those suitable for countries where *Phylloxera* is a pest):

'Cascade', black grape, red wine, vigorous grower for outside walls

'Black Hamburg', black grape, red wine, for greenhouse

'Buckland Sweetwater', green grape, white wine, for greenhouse

'Müller Thurgau', green grape, white wine, for outside

'Purpurea', decorative purple foliage, a non-vigorous grower for outside

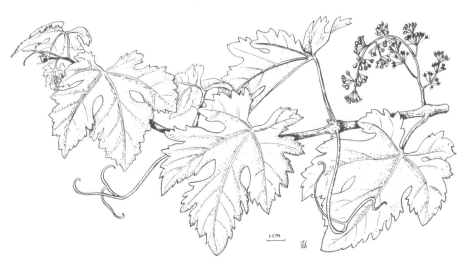

4
Large Trees

P. 74. Aleppo pine *Pinus halepensis* in Israel.

Large trees will take up a lot of space when fully grown. On the other hand, it will be many years before they reach full size and it may be well worthwhile growing them for a time, until they become too large for the site. It may be, too, that some of these forest trees could be grown in preference to other non-biblical ones which are already growing on or near the site of your Bible garden. Remarks on p. 43 on planting and pruning shrubs and small trees apply equally to large trees.

Pl. 75. A remnant forest of cedar of Lebanon *Cedrus libani* on Mount Lebanon.

Cedar (*Cedrus*)

For thousands of years Mount Lebanon has provided a rich source of timber for countries round about. King Solomon made arrangements with Hiram, King of Tyre on the coast of Lebanon (ancient Phoenicia), for the felling and transport of cedars and other timbers to Jerusalem (1 Kings 5:6,8,10; 2 Chronicles 2). It was there that Solomon built his great Temple to the Lord which endured for over 300 years until it was destroyed in 586 B.C. Cedar was used for making many other objects, such as furniture and ships; there are also several references to the beauty and strength of the tree (Amos 2:9).

The cedar of Lebanon is a coniferous tree with short needle leaves in clusters, living to a great age. Although young trees have the conical shape characteristic of Christmas trees, old specimens progressively develop a flat-topped appearance with horizontal branches and a massive trunk. The large cones with rounded tops stand erect on the branches until mature when they shatter to release their seeds.

Cultivation

The true cedar of Lebanon may be difficult to obtain from commercial nurseries; if so, there are alternatives which have similar features. However, beware of totally different plants which are popularly known as 'cedar' but have nothing to do with the genus *Cedrus*. The species listed below grow slowly but after some years develop into handsome trees. If you want yours to reach maturity choose a site large enough to accept a tree 30m (100ft) high with a similar spread. All the species are hardy but old trees may suffer broken branches in heavy snowfalls.

Fig 44. Cedar of Lebanon, *Cedrus libani*.

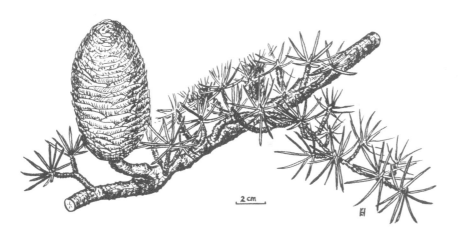

2 cm

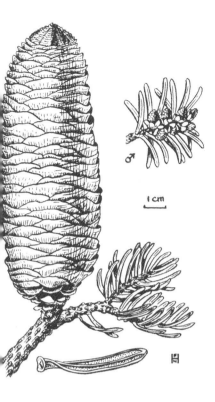

Cypress
(*Cupressus*)

The cypress tree is native in the Holy Land and surrounding countries and is undoubtedly mentioned several times in the Scriptures. It was evidently one of the timbers used for the construction of King Solomon's Temple at Jerusalem (1 Kings 9:11, as 'fir' KJV); its pleasant evergreen appearance attracted Isaiah's attention as he prophesied cypress growing in the desert (Isaiah 41:19); and some commentators even consider that the 'gopher wood' used for the construction of Noah's Ark was cypress (Genesis 6:14)

Cypress trees are also well known in gardens and cemeteries throughout temperate countries. There are several species and even hybrids which look similar. The close, evergreen foliage is composed of scale leaves which are quite resinous and fragrant. The fruits are round and knobbly, becoming dry cones.

Cultivation

Most species are hardy evergreen trees which can become very tall and slender in habit. When planted by itself a cypress tree will make a splendid feature, or several may be used as a screen or even a hedge. Plant in autumn or spring making sure the roots do not dry out afterwards. Fairly rich moist soil is preferred. They can be grown from seed or cuttings.

Fig. 46. Italian cypress *Cupressus sempervirens*, with scale-leaves, cones and a seed.

Fig. 45. Cilician fir *Abies cilicica*.

Species

Cedrus atlantica, Atlantic cedar, Atlas mountains; the var. *glauca* has silver-grey needle leaves and is widely cultivated

C. brevifolia, Cyprus cedar, Turkey and Cyprus, rarely seen in cultivation, very similar to cedar of Lebanon and often regarded as a form of it

C. deodara, deodar, Himalayas, often grown in large gardens, has a drooping habit with green needle leaves longer than those of other species

C. libani, cedar of Lebanon, the biblical species widely planted in Britain during the 18th century; such trees are now seen as stately specimens in large gardens and parks (see fig. 44 and pl. 75)

Abies cilicica, Cilician fir, grows in the Lebanon forests with cedar and was undoubtedly exploited with it; a tall stately tree (see fig. 45)

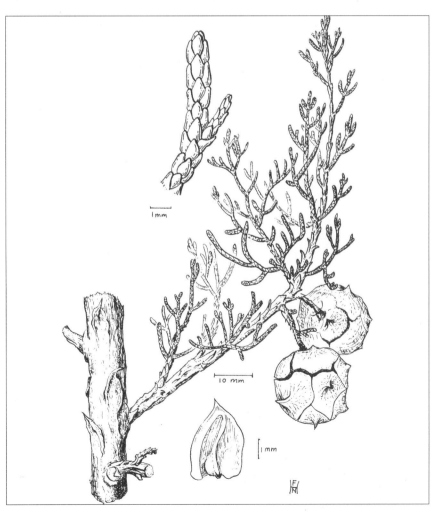

Pl. 76. Evergreen cypress *Cupressus sempervirens* on the Temple Mount, Jerusalem.

Walnut (*Juglans*)

There is one biblical reference to the walnut, although the name is not actually given in any English-language version: 'I went down to the nut orchard, to look at the blossoms of the valley, to see whether the vines had budded, whether the pomegranates were in bloom' (Song of Solomon 6:11).

The nuts are very familiar to most people even if the tree itself is not commonly known. The timber, too, is a favourite for the manufacture of fine furniture. In classical times the Greeks likened the crinkled appearance of the nut kernel to the brain, while the Romans called it Jupiter's nut, *Jovis glans*, from which the scientific name *Juglans* was derived. The English name 'walnut' is a corruption of 'the nut that came via Gaul'! The hard covering of the seed cracks open into two boatlike pieces, but nuts for pickling should be collected before they become hard.

Species

Cupressus lawsoniana (or *C. Chamaecyparis lawsoniana*), Lawson cypress, California and Oregon, commonly grown in gardens and rather similar to the Mediterranean tree but hardier

C. sempervirens, Italian or evergreen cypress, the biblical species often seen in Mediterranean countries where the slender (fastigiate) form is planted in graveyards; prefers warm climates although it will survive in southern England where its trunk remains flexible in wind and needs support (see fig. 46 and pl. 76)

Fig. 47. Common walnut *Juglans regia*, with female flower and a fruit.

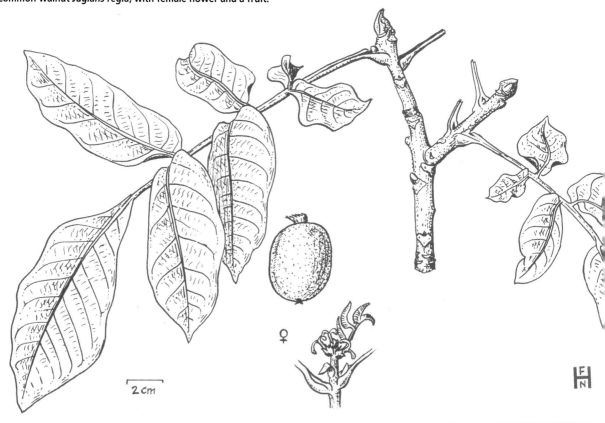

Pl. 78. Walnuts *Juglans*.

Pl. 77. Walnut Tree *Juglans regia*.

Juniper (*Juniperus*)

When Solomon became king of Israel he planned to build a temple in Jerusalem. He asked the King of Tyre for timber from the great forests on the mountains of Lebanon and men were sent to cut down the trees (1 Kings 5:3-6 and 9:11). These were not only the famous cedars of Lebanon but also cypress (*Cupressus*), fir (*Abies*), pine (*Pinus*) and juniper (*Juniperus*), all being conifers.

This juniper is the eastern savin (*J. excelsa*) which is a hardy tree growing with a narrowly pyramidal habit up to 15-20m (50-65ft). Although a conifer, like all junipers its fruits are not true cones but round and berry-like, becoming purplish brown. It has small, sharp-pointed evergreen leaves and stringy bark that peels off in strips. The whole tree is strongly fragrant owing to its resin.

The tender Phoenician juniper was the 'cedarwood' used in the Tabernacle rites (Leviticus 14:4,6).

Cultivation

It is best grown from seed as a young plant because walnuts do not take well to transplanting. Remember that it will grow to a large tree – not only high but also spreading widely – and it develops surprisingly quickly for a tree. Young shoots may be cut back during hard frosts but it is generally hardy and needs full sun.

Species

Juglans regia, common walnut, S.E. Europe to Central Asia, up to 25m (80ft) high, deciduous pinnate leaves, male and female inflorescences are wind-pollinated in early spring before the leaves appear (see fig. 47 and pls 77 and 78)

J. nigra, black walnut, USA, similar to the above and even taller, could be grown as a substitute; its nuts are inedible

Cultivation

Choose the site carefully to take advantage of the evergreen nature of this tree. It does not spread as widely as some others so it could be used as a background for lighter subjects. Plant in early spring rather than winter to avoid a check in growth and water well until established. Light or chalky soils are suitable.

Above: Pl. 79. Eastern savin *Juniperus excelsa*.
Below: Fig. 48. Eastern savin *Juniperus excelsa* in fruit.

Species

Juniperus excelsa, eastern savin, S.E. Europe to C. Asia (see fig. 48 and pl. 79)

J. virginiana, eastern red cedar, eastern USA and Canada, a similar tree to *J. excelsa* although originating on the other side of the Atlantic, and more readily available from nurseries; some cultivars are blue-grey in appearance

J. phoenicea, Phoenician juniper or 'cedarwood' of the Tabernacle rites, S. Europe to S.W. Asia and N. Africa, tender tree of dry conditions only suitable for a cool greenhouse or countries with a very mild winter

Pine Tree (*Pinus*)

Although several species of pine are conspicuous features of the scenery in the Mediterranean region, including the Holy Land, it is difficult to be sure whether they are actually mentioned in the Scriptures. However, pine timber must have been used in the construction of buildings such as the Temple in Jerusalem (1 Kings 6:15, New International Version) along with imported cedar of Lebanon (1 Kings 5:10). This would have been the wood of the Aleppo pine (*Pinus halepensis*) and the Brutian pine (*P. brutia*) which are similar coniferous trees with pairs of needle leaves and woody cones bearing winged seeds. However, the stone pine (*P. pinea*), which is thought to be the tree mentioned in Hosea 14:8: 'I am like an evergreen cypress; your faithfulness comes from me', has seeds which are edible and nut-like; it has an umbrella-like crown, and usually grows nearer the coast than the Aleppo pine.

Cultivation

Pines may be grown from seed, if you are prepared to wait for a few years until they develop into trees. Otherwise saplings of all sizes may be purchased from nurseries and garden centres

Pl. 80. Stone pine *Pinus pinea*.

They thrive in any soil, especially if it is light and sandy (where they must be watered to become established). Avoid at all costs cutting the leading stem or a malformed tree will result: even established trees should not be lopped or they will look unsightly. Plant where there is sufficient room for them to grow. Being evergreen, pines can be used as a screen for buildings or as a windbreak in exposed positions. Almost any species of pine having two-needle leaves together, could be used, depending on availability, and a few are mentioned below: the Mediterranean species are reasonably hardy.

Species

Pinus brutia, Brutian pine, Lebanon and Turkey, 15m (50ft)

P. halepensis, Aleppo or Jerusalem pine, E. Mediterranean region, 15m (50ft) (see pl. 74, fig. 49)

P. pinaster, cluster pine, W. Mediterranean region, 30-37m (100-120 ft) – substitute species

P. pinea, stone or umbrella pine, Mediterranean region, 12-27m (40-90ft) having edible seeds (see pl. 80)

P. sylvestris, Scots pine, Europe, 15-30m (50-100ft) – substitute species

P. thunbergii, black pine, Japan, 24-30m (80-100 ft) – substitute species

Fig. 49. Aleppo pine *Pinus halepensis* with cones.

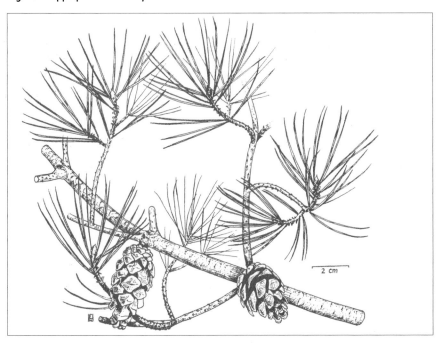

2 cm

Plane Tree (*Platanus*)

When Jacob was working for his uncle Laban he is said to have encouraged the flock to breed speckled progeny by peeling strips of bark from branches of several trees, including those of the plane tree (Genesis 30:37), and setting them in the watering troughs where the flocks came to drink. The plane tree is also mentioned in Ezekiel 31:8 and Isaiah 41:19, 60:13.

In the Holy Land oriental plane trees grow along streams where they develop into very large trees. They have characteristic trunks as the bark flakes off leaving irregular bare patches. The large leaves are digitately lobed and coarsely papery when they fall in the autumn, and they take a long time to rot. The individual flowers are insignificant; the male and female are borne in separate clusters suspended on a long stalk, the female developing in balls that eventually break up into plumed seeds.

Fig. 50. Eastern plane *Platanus orientalis* in fruit.

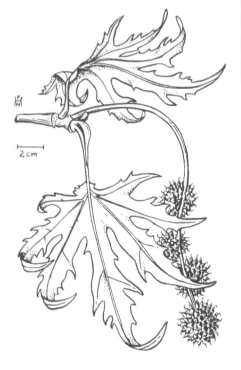

Pl. 81. Eastern plane *tree Platanus orientalis*.

Cultivation

As a streamside species plane trees need plenty of moisture. Seeds germinate readily outside and grow rapidly in a sunny situation. Ultimately the trees become immense and this should be borne in mind before planting one.

Species

Platanus x hispanica (*P. acerifolia*), London plane, probably a hybrid between the two following species and widely planted in cities where it does better than either of its parents, two to four fruit balls on each stalk

P. occidentalis, western plane, the 'sycamore' of USA, a huge tree, a substitute for the next species, sometimes cultivated in Europe, usually one fruit ball on each stalk

P. orientalis, eastern plane, S.E. Europe-W. Asia, the biblical tree, two to six fruit balls on each stalk (see fig. 50 and pl. 81)

Poplar (*Populus*) and Willow (*Salix*)

Some species of willow and poplar are streamside trees and this habitat is mentioned in Leviticus 23:40 ('willows of the brook') and Isaiah 44:3-4 ('willows by flowing streams'). The willows of the Holy Land have long narrow leaves like the others listed below which may be used as substitutes in a Bible garden if you have space.

There is considerable confusion in the various translations of the Bible between willows and poplars. The New International Version is correct in rendering the famous passage in Psalm 137:1-3, 'By the rivers of Babylon we sat and wept when we remembered Zion. There on the poplars we hung our harps,' where other versions use 'the willows'. This is the Euphrates poplar, while the white poplar is probably the one Jacob peeled in order to encourage his father-in-law's sheep to breed speckled lambs (Genesis 30:37) (see *Styrax*, p. 49).

Pl. 82. Euphrates poplar *Populus euphratica.*

Pl. 83. White poplar *Populus alba.*

Fig. 51. Euphrates poplar *Populus euphratica*, A young leaves, B male flowers, C female flowers, D mature leaves and fruits.

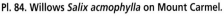

Pl. 84. Willows *Salix acmophylla* on Mount Carmel.

Cultivation

Both willows and poplars are easily grown from cuttings in moist soil. In spite of their natural habitat being wet, the trees will grow in ordinary garden soil, but if you have space beside water they will look more effective (see Chapter 5: Water plants). They may be pollarded successfully when they become too large.

Species

Populus alba, white poplar, Europe and W. Asia, 15m (50ft) or more (see pl. 83)

P. canescens, grey poplar, Europe, 21m (70ft), similar to white poplar

P. euphratica, Euphrates poplar, Middle East, shrub or small tree (see fig. 51 and pl. 82)

P. nigra, black poplar, Europe, very large tree with more spreading habit than the Lombardy poplar (var. *italica*)

Salix acmophylla (see pl. 84) and *S. alba*, the willow species of the Holy Land

S. babylonica (and hybrid *S.* 'Chrysocoma'), weeping willow, China in spite of its supposed origin in Babylon

S. fragilis, crack willow, and *S. viminalis*, osier, both European with narrow leaves, up to 20m (65ft) high

Oak Tree (*Quercus*)

In biblical times there were oak woodlands both on the hills and in the plains, where nowadays at best there may be a residual tree or a cemetery grove. The practice of burying the dead under oaks is referred to when Deborah, Rebekah's nurse, was buried under one (Genesis 35:8). The shade of an oak tree is a good place to sit (1 Kings 13:14), its timber is excellent for ships (Ezekiel 27:6) and strong (Amos 2:9). Sacred groves (or Asherim poles) were places of idolatry and immoral worship (2 Kings 23:14). Even the scale insects infesting oaks were used to provide the scarlet dye with which the Israelites dyed wool and skins for the priests' garments (Exodus 35:23). In Bible translations oaks and terebinth trees are often confused (see p. 88).

Mediterranean oaks are either deciduous or evergreen. They vary in size, from small bushes to large trees, with gnarled trunks and spreading branches when they become old. Some species have quite prickly leaves, others are lobed. The nuts are popularly known as acorns and sit in a little cup which in the Holy Land oaks is bristly.

Cultivation

'He who plants an oak plants for his grandchildren': maybe, but a nice little tree can grow in your own lifetime. The acorns soon die if dried, so sow them while fresh. Transplanted saplings may be difficult to establish if the roots are cut in lifting, therefore it is best to plant a seedling or to cut down the stem of a sapling on planting and wait for a new shoot to grow. Evergreen oaks can be grown as a hedge or as rounded single trees but

Pl. 85. Palestinian oak *Quercus calliprinos*, a form of *Q. cocccifera*, the Kermes oak.

they are not hardy enough for countries with cold winters, such as occur in Central Europe. Almost any species of oak would be acceptable for your Bible garden; the following list selects a few alternatives.

Species

Q. coccifera (including *Q. calliprinos*), Kermes or Palestinian oak, Mediterranean, evergreen glossy prickly leaves, often shrubby, as a small tree grows up to 4m (12ft) high (see fig. 52 and pl. 85)

Q. ilex, holm oak or ilex, W. Mediterranean, evergreen, a possible substitute for the Kermes oak and making a larger tree

Q. macrolepis (*Q. aegilops*, *Q. ithaburensis*) Valonia or Tabor oak, E. Mediterranean, deciduous, up to 20m (66ft) high and nearly as wide

Q. robur, English oak, Europe, deciduous, a possible substitute for the Tabor oak.

Fig. 52. Palestinian oak *Quercus calliprinos*, male and female flowers.

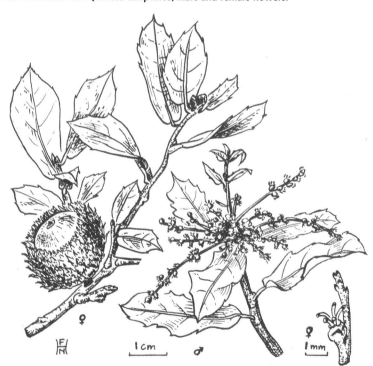

5
Water Plants

Pl. 86. Great reed-mace *Typha latifolia.*

A pool or stream is a very attractive feature in any garden and widens the scope for planting. Should you be fortunate enough to possess one or other already, you can easily adapt it to take biblical plants. Most people, though, will need to create a pool from scratch. Nowadays there are several aids which make the proposition easy and successful, namely the availability of moulded plastic and glass-fibre pool bases. There are two main types – rigid and pliable. The rigid ones can be fitted into a hole of the appropriate size and depth, while the pliable type is more adaptable and enables you to create additional features. Full instructions come with each type. Whichever is chosen, the landscaping of the edges and surrounds can make or mar the overall effect. A suitable paving, at least on one side of the pool, is necessary to enable you to approach it closely; you can help to ameliorate the abrupt lines by using overlapping plants on the other side. However, avoid siting the pool in a shady place as most water plants need plenty of light, and in any case overhanging trees will drop their leaves into the water, which is a nuisance.

It is important to provide both deeper water for submerged aquatics, like water-lilies, and shallow muddy places for marsh plants. If you decide on a rigid pool, choose one which makes allowance for this; if you pick the pliable type, lay it over suitable contours so when it is filled with water there are variable depths.

Planting of roots is best done when the water is not too cold and the growing season is beginning (May in Europe and North America). Strongly growing species can be restricted by planting these in submerged containers .

There may be an excessive growth of green algae if fertiliser is allowed to pollute the water. Another problem can be the breeding of mosquitoes in a stagnant pool, but this is easily dealt with by introducing suitable fish which will dispose of the larvae. Mosquitoes will be deterred by circulating the water with a concealed electric pump. A pool is more interesting if it includes fish and other creatures in a well-balanced way and it will be an attraction to birds too. A word of warning should be given, however: a pool in a place which is frequented by small children can be dangerous.

See the list on p. 92 of references for books on the subject.

Sweet Flag, Aromatic Cane (*Acorus*)

Some readers of the Bible have assumed that the aromatic, fragrant or sweet cane (calamus) mentioned in Exodus (30:23) and the Song of Solomon (4:14) was the sugar cane, but this was not known in biblical lands at that period. In those days there was in the spice trade a fragrant, cane-like rhizome that was carried in the dry state by animal caravans from Central Asia. It was used in the holy anointing oil and for special perfumery. We now know that it was the rhizome of the sweet flag (*Acorus calamus*).

This is a waterside plant that could easily be mistaken for an iris, but it belongs to a very different family – the arum or lords-and-ladies family, *Araceae*. During the summer its inconspicuous yellow-green flowerheads may be seen low down among the leaves. The fragrant sword-like leaves die down in winter.

Fig. 53. Sweet flag *Acorus calamus*, with portions of fresh and dry rhizomes.

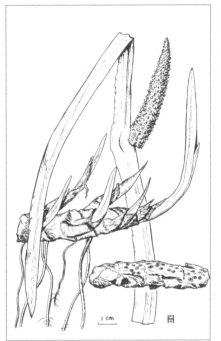

Pl. 87. Yellow flag *Iris pseudacorus*.

Cultivation

The sweet flag is hardy and easily grown in mud beside lakes or pools. Plant the rhizomes in early summer in mud or very shallow water. If they grow well and begin to crowd out neighbouring water-plants, it may be necessary to dig them up, thin out and replant. They can also be grown in tubs or large pots of rich soil kept moist by standing them in water.

Species

Acorus calamus, sweet flag, originally from Central Asia but now naturalised or planted in shallow water in many parts of the temperate world (see fig. 53)

Iris pseudacorus, yellow flag or iris, Europe and W. Asia including the Holy Land, decorative hardy strong-grower forming large clumps, 1-1.5m (3-5ft), a substitute for or an associate of sweet flag in a garden pool (see pl. 87)

Papyrus (*Cyperus*)

It is probable that much of the Bible was written on sheets of papyrus, and indeed our word 'paper' is derived from the Greek name for the pith of the sedge from which the writing material was made. The long spongy stalks of the papyrus plant were also used in Ancient Egypt for skiffs and boats of various sizes, referred to in Isaiah 18:2: '. . . sending ambassadors by the Nile in vessels of papyrus on the waters!'

At one time the Nile Delta was covered with papyrus – though it has now disappeared owing to agriculture and the drying up of the swamps. It is a tall sedge with a great mop-like flowerhead of thin green bracts and chaffy flowers.

Fig. 54. Papyrus *Cyperus papyrus*.

Top: Pl. 88. Papyrus swamp; bottom: Pl. 89. Papyrus with water-lily.

It still grows wild in Lake Huleh in Israel and is now cultivated in Egypt for making papyrus sheets to sell to tourists.

Cultivation

As papyrus is a tropical or subtropical marsh-plant, it needs warm conditions and standing water. It can be grown outside in southern Europe but further north it requires a greenhouse with enough headroom. The stout rhizomes should be planted in mud in shallow water.

A popular substitute for the true papyrus is the umbrella sedge (which is often erroneously called papyrus) as it will tolerate less tropical conditions. It grows well in a small pot of compost soil, standing in a bowl of water, either indoors in a sunny window, or outside beside a pool in summer only as it will not tolerate frost. Propagation is by division of the roots, or by floating the flowerhead in water until roots appear, or by seeds scattered on warm damp soil (20°C, 68°F) in spring.

Species

Cyperus papyrus, papyrus or Egyptian paper sedge, tropical Africa, Israel (Huleh swamp), Sicily (Syracuse); 3-4m (10-13 ft) (see fig. 54 and pls. 88, 89)

C. alternifolius, umbrella sedge, or umbrella grass, or false papyrus, E. Africa, 1m (3-4ft); var. *gracilis*, dwarf, 30-45cm (12-18in.); var. *variegatus*, with green and yellow stripes

Water-lily (*Nymphaea*)

Although water-lilies are not mentioned by name in the Bible, there is little doubt that water-lily flowers inspired the form of the capitals at the top of the two bronze columns in the vestibule of Solomon's Temple (2 Chronicles 3:16) and the Temple furnishings (2 Chronicles 4:5). The water-lily was much better known in Egypt, where it grew in backwaters of the Nile, than in Canaan, but the Israelite craftsmen would have been familiar with the Egyptian motif that must have inspired the form of the capitals. In Ancient Egyptian temples, water-lily (or 'lotus') capitals featured on many columns, and the flower was actually the symbol of Upper Egypt. (Much later the name 'lotus' was applied to the Asian water-lily *Nelumbo nucifera* which holds its leaves and flowers much higher above the water than *Nymphaea*.)

There are two wild Egyptian species of *Nymphaea*: *N. lotus* and *N. caerulea*. The former is white-flowered, opening in late afternoon and closing about eleven o'clock on the following morning. *N. caerulea* is a smaller plant with blue flowers that open from about seven in the morning until one o'clock, and they are sweetly fragrant –

Pl. 90. White Egyptian lotus water-Lily *Nymphaea lotus.*

hence Egyptian murals often depict Pharaoh or his officials smelling flowers of the blue water-lily.

Cultivation

Subtropical water-lilies need to be grown in a warm pool 30-60cm (1-2ft) deep where the rhizomes can be submerged in tubs of warm compost. In temperate countries this means they will have to be grown in a greenhouse pool at 18-21°C (65-70°F). However, owners of sunny outside pools can use similar white-flowered species to good effect. Although no hardy blue-flowered species is known, tender plants could be put outside during the summer months. Hybrids in many beautiful colours are more easily available than true species. Propagation is by seeds sown in water, but the purchase of rhizomes is recommended.

Species

Nymphaea caerulea, blue Egyptian lotus water-lily, Egypt

N. lotus, white Egyptian lotus water-lily, Africa (see fig. 55 and pl. 90)

Hardy species
N. alba, white, Europe including Britain
N. candida, white, Central Europe
N. fennica, white, Finland
N. odorata, white, North America
N. tetragona, white, Himalayas
N. tuberosa, white, North America

Tender species
N. blanda, white, South America
N. capensis, blue, South Africa
N. gigantea, blue, Australia
N. gracilis, white, Mexico
N. stellata, blue, India

Fig. 55. White Egyptian lotus water-lily *Nymphaea lotus.*

Top: Pl. 91. Giant reed *Arundo donax*; bottom: Pl. 92. Common reed *Phragmites australis*.

Reeds (*Arundo, Phragmites*)

Several waterside plants are mentioned in the Bible and the well-known common reed is one of them. It has bamboo-like canes which shake in the water as the wind blows over them (1 Kings 14:15). The canes are not strong and the phrase 'a broken reed' of 2 Kings 18:21 has passed into everyday English for a weak supporter. In ancient biblical days short lengths of reed were cut for use as arrows (Psalm 120:4), as pens (3 John:13) and as measuring rods (Ezekiel 40:5). The rhizomes of this grass creep in the water forming reed-beds where there is plenty of space, and the brownish plumes develop in late summer on top of the canes which grow taller than a man.

Cultivation

The common reed is a vigorous grower and could quickly take over a small pool unless restricted by growing it in a submerged tub. Plant rhizomes in early spring in shallow water or wet mud where growth will be less vigorous. Alternatively, the giant reed (*Arundo donax*) could be used as it tolerates ordinary garden soil provided it is fairly moist.

Species

Arundo donax, giant reed, Mediterranean region, stout white plumed canes up to 3m (10ft) (see pl. 91)

Phragmites australis (formerly known as *P. communis*), common reed, reed grass, worldwide, canes over 2m (7ft) (see fig. 56 and pl. 92)

Fig. 56. Common reed *Phragmites australis*.

Ancient coiled basket with lid, made of papyrus.

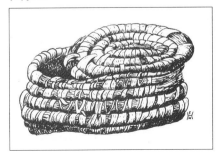

Pl. 93. Bulrush *Scirpus lacustris.*

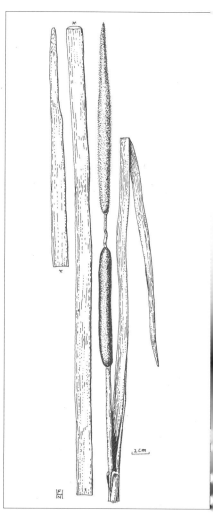

Fig. 57. Reed-mace *Typha domingensis.*

Reed-Mace, Cat-Tail, Bulrush (*Typha*)

One of the most famous stories known to almost everybody is the finding of baby Moses floating in a cradle in the River Nile (Exodus 2:3-5). He had been placed there by his mother to avoid his being murdered on the orders of Pharaoh ('Every boy that is born to the Hebrews you shall throw into the Nile') as he did not want Hebrew boys to live. The cradle floated among the waterside cat-tails, bulrushes and reeds, and was found and rescued by Pharaoh's daughter when she came down to bathe.

The name 'bulrush' should strictly be used for a tall sedge known as *Scirpus lacustris* which does grow in the lakes and pools in Egypt, but it is often intended for the cat-tail or reed-mace (*Typha*) referred to in the Bible passage. There are several quite similar species that could be grown instead of the Egyptian *T. domingensis*. They all have long strap-like leaves and tall stalks carrying the characteristic cylindrical brown flowerheads with male and female flowers separated, one below the other. They are often used in dried flower arrangements.

Cultivation

A pool or slow-running stream with plenty of mud would be ideal for growing *Typha*. It is a strong grower and could soon crowd out weaker species, so if you wish to restrict growth, in spring plant the rhizomes into a submerged pot filled with mud, instead of directly into the pool.

Species

Typha angustifolia, lesser reed-mace or cat-tail, Europe, N. America and Asia

T. domingensis (formerly *T. australis*), tropics and subtropics including Egypt (see fig. 57)

T. latifolia, great reed-mace, N. temperate region to tropical Africa and throughout N. and S. America (see pl. 86)

Scirpus lacustris, bulrush, N. temperate and Mediterranean regions, 2m (6ft), small sedge-like flowerheads (see pl. 93)

6
Tender Plants

Pl. 94. Date palm *Phoenix dactylifera*.

The inclusion of tender species widens the scope for the enthusiast with a garden in a suitable climate or with a greenhouse. It may also encourage you to grow such plants on window-sills inside your home during the winter, moving them outside when the weather is warm enough. While some of the species are tolerant of a wide range of temperatures, others need constant warmth, as will be seen from the notes. The availability of some of these plants is very doubtful as they occur in remote parts of the world and are rarely in cultivation. But if you *can* obtain them, they are fascinating to grow.

Pl. 95. Acacia tree *Acacia tortilis* subspecies *raddiana*.

Acacia Tree
(*Acacia*)

Very few species of trees occur in the Sinai desert where Moses wandered with the people of Israel. It was no wonder, therefore, that the portable Tent of Meeting (or Tabernacle) was constructed of acacia wood, called *shittim* in Hebrew and left untranslated in the King James (Authorised) Version. Detailed instructions were provided by God for its construction by the joiner Bezaleel who also made the furniture of acacia wood (Exodus 25:10 onwards; 37:1 onwards).

Acacias occur in the desert mainly along the wadis which are the dry water courses that flow occasionally after freak storms. Typically, acacias are small, flat-topped trees with extremely prickly branches and small compound leaves, heads of yellow flowers, and brown pods. The timber is hard and brown. Some acacias exude the resin gum arabic.

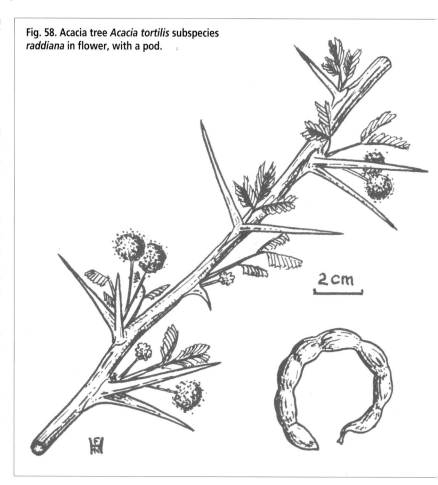

Fig. 58. Acacia tree *Acacia tortilis* subspecies *raddiana* in flower, with a pod.

2 cm

Cultivation

Being trees of tropical or subtropical deserts they will not grow outside in temperate countries – where a warm greenhouse is essential – but in warm countries they grow quickly and make fine trees, giving light shade. It is best to raise them from seeds, though these are not easy to obtain and are often riddled with insects.

An alternative to the true biblical acacia is one of the numerous Australian acacias, but this is stretching the association considerably since many have flattened leaf-stalks (phyllodes) and belong to an entirely different group of species from the Middle Eastern acacias. A species with finely divided leaves is *A. dealbata*, the silver wattle or mimosa, New South Wales to Tasmania, a well-known ornamental which flourishes outside in mild regions but may succumb in severe winters. It is available from nurseries.

Species

Acacia tortilis subspecies *raddiana* (or *A. raddiana*), the true acacia tree of Sinai; for an alternative see above (see fig. 58 and pl. 95).

Other biblical tropical timbers include:

Dalbergia melanoxylon, African ebony or blackwood, the ebony of Ancient Egypt occurring in dry country south of the Sahara and may have been imported by Solomon's fleet (2 Chronicles 9:10 'algum') and later traders (Ezekiel 27:15)

Diospyros ebenum, Ceylon ebony, used nowadays and doubtfully in Old Testament times

Pterocarpus santolinus, red sandalwood or saunders, of tropical Asia, some consider to be algum (almug) of 2 Chronicles 9:10

Aloes
(*Aloe, Aquilaria*)

After the death of Jesus on the Cross, Joseph of Arimathea, a secret disciple, asked Pilate for permission to bury him, and a Jewish leader, named Nicodemus, 'who had at first come to Jesus by night', brought a mixture of myrrh and aloes, 'weighing about a hundred pounds'. Together they took the body of Jesus 'and wrapped it with the spices in linen cloths according to the burial custom of the Jews' (John 19:39-40).

The aloe plant is short-stemmed with a tuft of succulent leaves which have very sharp teeth along their edges and end in a point. The tall spikes of yellowish flowers develop in early spring. Aloe juice is very bitter (it is enjoying a resurgence of popularity as a medicine).

Pl. 96. Bitter aloes *Aloe vera.*

The fragrant aloes of Psalm 45:8 were obtained from timber of the lign-aloe tree, *Aquilaria*, a totally different species.

Cultivation

Off-sets grow readily outside in dry situations in warm countries. Elsewhere they need to be grown inside as house plants where they should be given plenty of light, but not scorched, with occasional watering.

Lign-aloe needs a humid tropical environment.

Species

Aloe vera (also called *A. barbadensis*), the true species originally from the Yemen and now grown widely; there are many similar species in tropical and southern Africa (see fig. 59 and pl. 96)

Aquilaria agallocha, eaglewood or lign-aloe, N. India, unlikely to be cultivated or obtainable

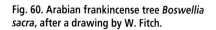

Frankincense (*Boswellia*)

Incense or frankincense was burnt as a fragrant perfume by Jewish priests in religious ceremonies (Leviticus 16:12) and it was one of the treasures brought to the infant Jesus by the wise men (Matthew 2:11). It is a resin obtained from incisions in the trunk of *Boswellia* trees which inhabit dry mountains in the Horn of Africa and southern Arabia. Frankincense was exported from Sheba in S.W. Arabia (1 Kings 10:10; Isaiah 60:6).

Cultivation

It would be most unusual to be able to include a frankincense tree in a collection of biblical plants, though given suitable conditions, the trees will grow from seeds or cuttings – themselves difficult to obtain. Make sure they do not rot at the roots by being too moist.

Fig. 59. Bitter aloe *Aloe vera* with a flower.

Fig. 60. Arabian frankincense tree *Boswellia sacra*, after a drawing by W. Fitch.

Above: Pl. 97. Frankincense resin.
Below: Pl. 98. Frankincense trees *Boswellia sacra* growing on a rock in Somalia.

Species

Boswellia sacra, S. Arabia and Somalia, bush or tree 2-10m (6-30ft) high (see fig. 60 and pls 97 and 98)

B. thurifera, India, small tree

Caperbush (*Capparis*)

On linguistic grounds there is good reason for believing that this is the plant referred to as 'desire' in the following verse: 'The almond tree blossoms, the grasshopper drags itself along and desire fails; because all must go to their eternal home, and the mourners will go about the streets' (Ecclesiastes 12:5). It is also said to be 'the hyssop that grows in the wall' spoken of by Solomon (1 Kings 4:33) since the caperbush is frequently seen on old buildings in the Mediterranean area, rooted between the stones (see also 'hyssop' under marjoram p. 38 and sorghum p. 25). Its slender trailing stems bear sharp stipular spines and rounded leather leaves; the flowers are large and spectacular with numerous

Fig. 61. Caperbush *Capparis spinosa* habit, flower and fruit.

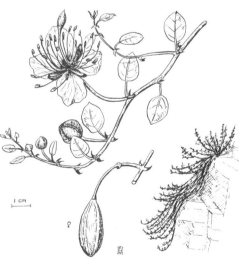

Pl. 99. Caperbush *Capparis spinosa*.

long stamens protruding widely. Flower buds are pickled as capers.

Cultivation

Suitable for warm countries outside in full sun and dry soil, or in a cool greenhouse where it does best in well-drained pots. Cuttings root in sand at high temperatures.

Species

Capparis spinosa, caperbush, Mediterranean region, flowers open during the night, white tinged lilac (see fig. 61 and pl. 99)

Carob, St John's Bread, 'Locusts' (*Ceratonia*)

In the Parable of the Prodigal Son Jesus pictured the lad who had squandered his money on loose living having to keep pigs – a terrible occupation for a Jew who regards them as unclean animals. Moreover, during a time of famine he had to share the pigs' food, pods of the carob tree (Luke 15:16). Actually, these are sweet and wholesome and nowadays are used in health foods! Some commentators hold that they were the 'locusts' John the Baptist ate in the desert, hence the name 'St John's bread', but these equally could have been the insects (Matthew 3:4).

Above: **Pl. 100.** Carob or locust bean tree *Ceratonia siliqua*.

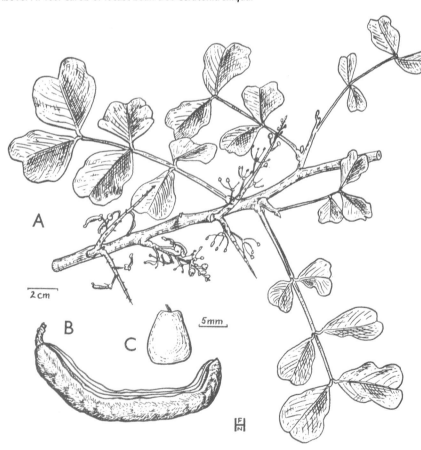

Right: **Fig. 62.** Carob *Ceratonia siliqua*, with pod and a seed.

Cultivation

They grow easily from seeds (even commercially available pods may have viable seeds) and they develop into rounded bushes or small evergreen trees which need to be grown in a warm sheltered position outside, with protection in winter, or in a cool greenhouse. Cuttings root better with bottom heat, and seeds are best soaked before sowing.

Species

Ceratonia siliqua, carob or locust bean, St John's bread, Holy Land and Mediterranean area, inconspicuous male and female pea flowers on different trees, appearing on trunk and branches in autumn, the pods maturing a year later (see fig. 62 and pl. 100)

Above: Pl. 101. Cinnamon *Cinnamomum verum*, photographed in Sri Lanka.

Below: Fig. 63. Cinnamon *Cinnamomum verum*. A flowering shoot, B flower bud, C anthers and cinnamon bark sticks.

Cinnamon, Cassia (*Cinnamomum*)

'Take the finest spices: of liquid myrrh five hundred shekels, and of sweet-smelling cinnamon half as much, that is, two hundred and fifty, and two hundred and fifty of aromatic cane, and five hundred of cassia . . .' (Exodus 30:23,24). These were the instructions the Lord gave to Moses for making the sacred oil blended by a perfumer for anointing the holy place and the priests. We cannot be sure that the cinnamon and cassia of ancient times were the same plant products we know today. These are both obtained from the bark of members of the genus *Cinnamomum* in the laurel family, *Lauraceae*. Although growing in different areas of the Far East they both have leathery leaves with prominent nerves arising from the end of the stalk.

Cultivation

Hot, humid conditions are necessary for these evergreen tropical species.

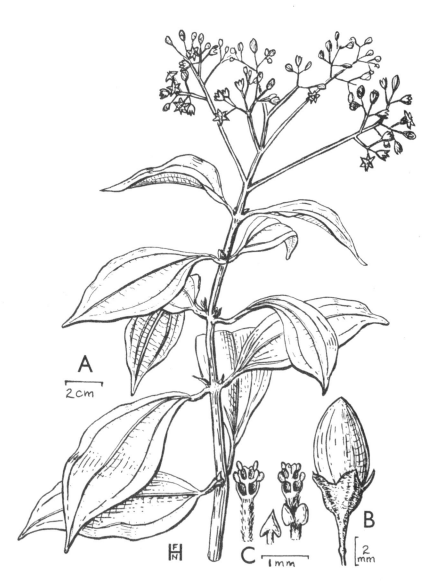

They may be grown from cuttings and thrive in well-watered, peaty soil with good drainage. Avoid disturbing the roots by transplanting.

Species

Cinnamomum cassia, cassia bark tree, S. China, tree up to 10m (30ft)

C. verum (*C. zeylanicum*), cinnamon tree, India and Sri Lanka (Ceylon), small tree or more usually shrubby (see fig. 63 and pl. 101)

Myrrh, Balm-of-Gilead (*Commiphora*)

Myrrh was also used for the sacred oil (Exodus 30:23, see notes on cinnamon) and like frankincense was offered to the infant Jesus (Matthew 2:11). It was obtained from species of a tropical shrub in the genus *Commiphora* which belongs to the same family as frankincense. Another species of *Commiphora* yields the balm (Ezekiel 27:17) or spices (1 Kings 10:10) now commonly

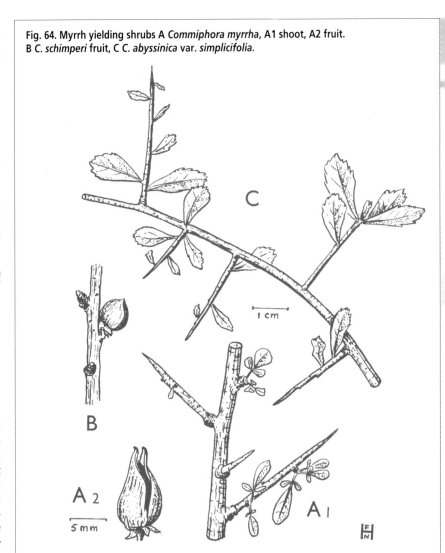

Fig. 64. Myrrh yielding shrubs A *Commiphora myrrha*, A1 shoot, A2 fruit. B *C. schimperi* fruit, C *C. abyssinica* var. *simplicifolia*.

Pl. 102. Balm-of-Gilead *Commiphora gileadensis* growing on hills in Yemen.

Fig. 65. Balm-of-Gilead *Commiphora gileadensis*.

Pl. 103. Myrrh tree *Commiphora myrrha*, photographed in Yemen.

Spikenard, Nard (*Cymbopogon, Nardostachys*)

'While the king was on his couch, my nard gave forth its fragrance,' says the Song of Solomon (1:12) clearly indicating an expensive perfume. This may have been the essential oil of the desert camel-grass (*Cymbopogon schoenanthus*). On the other hand, in the New Testament (John 12:3) we read how Jesus was anointed by Mary with pure nard (or spikenard) which is considered to be from *Nardostachys jatamansi*, a rare member of the Valerian family growing in the Himalayas.

Fig. 66. Camel grass *Cymbopogon schoenanthus*.

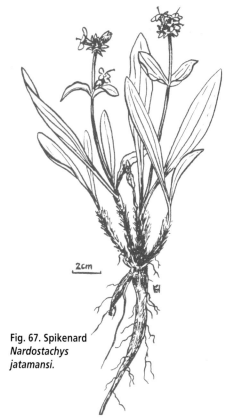

Fig. 67. Spikenard *Nardostachys jatamansi*.

known as balm-of-Gilead. These fragrant resins are still obtained by making incisions in the stems of these shrubs.

Cultivation

There are many species of *Commiphora* in Africa and Arabia where they inhabit dry country. Cuttings strike easily and seeds, if obtainable, may germinate. Grow in well-drained sandy soil, keeping temperature above 16°C (61°F) and with maximum light. However, it is seldom that a collection of biblical plants will be able to include them.

Species

Commiphora myrrha, myrrh tree, N.E. Africa and S.W. Africa, spiny (see fig. 64 and pl. 103)

C. gileadensis (or *C. opobalsamum*), balm-of-Gilead, N.E. Africa and S.W. Arabia, spineless, flowers tiny green, fruits small red berries (see fig 65 and pl. 102)

Cultivation

Cymbopogon schoenanthus (see fig. 66) should not be confused with the lemon grass, *C. citratus* from India, nor the *C. nardus* from Java, although these could be used as substitutes for the camel-grass from N. Africa to India. They need a warm greenhouse or hot conditions outside; growing tufted, they are decorative grasses 30-60cm (1-2ft) high with fragrant leaves. Lemon grass makes a tasty tisane (tea).

Nardostachys jatamansi is not a tropical plant as it occurs at high altitudes (see fig. 67). If seed cannot be obtained, substitute another member of the Valerian family such as red valerian, *Centranthus ruber*, which is a widespread perennial in Europe and grows easily from seed in ordinary soil, alkaline cliffs or old walls.

Species

Cymbopogon schoenanthus, camel-grass, Iraq desert grass (see fig. 66)

Nardostachys jatamansi, nard valerian, Himalayas (see fig. 67)

Pl. 104. Cotton bolls *Gossypium herbaceum.*

Cotton (*Gossypium*)

Today cotton cloth is so commonly used that it is hard to realise that it is not a very ancient material in the western world, although it has long been known in India. There is a possible biblical reference to cotton in Esther 1:6, which mentions the curtains hanging in the palace at Susa.

The cotton plant is a tropical shrub up to 2m (6ft) high, with lobed leaves and large, yellow, red-centred flowers like those of hollyhock, developing the capsule (the boll) with white-woolly seeds. The genus *Gossypium* belongs to the mallow family, *Malvaceae.*

Cultivation

Sow seeds in warm soil in spring, transplant seedlings first into small pots, finally into larger ones, or plant out if the climate is suitable, with temperatures 18°C (65°F) or above, with plenty of water in humus-rich soil.

Species

Gossypium herbaceum, Levant cotton, India to East Indies (see pl. 104)

Fig. 68. Henna *Lawsonia inermis* with fruits and a seed.

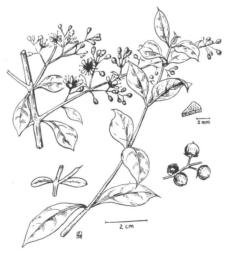

Henna (*Lawsonia*)

It is not surprising that the Song of Solomon (1:14) refers to henna blossoms growing at En-gedi, the hot oasis above the Dead Sea, as it is a tropical shrub. Its delicate white flowers have a delightful fragrance and in Arab countries a dye is still prepared from its crushed leaves to colour nails and hair yellow. It is a member of the loosestrife family, *Lythraceae.*

Cultivation

Hot dry conditions are required. Propagation is by cuttings in sandy peat.

Species

Lawsonia inermis, henna, N. Africa to India, shrub or small tree with many stems 2-3m (6-10ft) high (see fig. 68 and pl. 105)

Pl. 105. Henna *Lawsonia inermis.*

Oleander (*Nerium*)

In spite of this beautiful shrub being conspicuous along streams in the Holy Land where I have seen it on Carmel, in the Upper Jordan valley and at Petra, it is not mentioned in the Bible (it may occur in the Apocrypha, Ecclesiasticus 24:14, as the 'rose-bushes in Jericho', and as a place-name, 2 Esdras 9:26). However, it should be included in your Bible garden if possible. It grows as an evergreen, many-stemmed bush 2-3m (6-10ft) high with pink flowers. Beware of the leaves which are very poisonous to animals and people, so keep it away from children, avoiding contact with the white juice.

Cultivation

Oleanders need plenty of warm sunshine to ripen the young growths which produce the flowers later in the season. Trim back old growth to encourage production of new shoots. Keep well watered. If your climate is too cold for open-air cultivation grow oleanders in tubs which may be stood outside during the summer.

Species

Nerium oleander, oleander or rose-bay, Mediterranean area (see pl. 106)

Pl. 106. Oleander *Nerium oleander*.

Date Palm (*Phoenix*)

Jericho was called 'the city of palm trees' (Deuteronomy 34:3) and in Sinai at Elim, where the Israelites camped on the journey to the Promised Land, there were sev-

Pl. 107. Date palm *Phoenix dactylifera*.

enty palm trees growing by twelve springs of water (Numbers 33:9). Date palms flourish in hot conditions in desert oases, but they also grow in the hill country where Deborah lived (Judges 4:5), and in Jerusalem where leaves ('branches') were cut to welcome Jesus (John 12:13).

This tall unbranched palm has huge feather-like leaves with very sharp points and yields sweet fruits (dates).

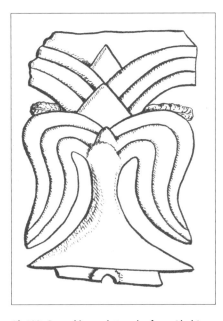

Pl. 108. Carved ivory date palm from Ahab's palace at Samaria (after *PEQ* 1933).

Pl. 109. Palestine terebinth *Pistacia terebinthus (P. palaestina)*.

Cultivation

Successful outdoor cultivation can only be achieved in hot countries. Male and female trees will be needed in order to obtain fruits – basal suckers from a female tree should be planted, as seeds will yield too many male trees. Plants raised from seeds sown in a warm place may be grown in containers inside a house or church for some years, until they become too large. I grow seeds (stones) from household dates, re-potting them when necessary. The leaf tips are very sharp!

Species

Phoenix dactylifera, date palm, Middle East, up to 21m (70ft) high (see pls 94, 107 and 108)

P. canariensis, Canary Islands date palm, a substitute for the true date, not as tall but with a stouter trunk and often planted along roads

Terebinth, Pistachio (*Pistacia*)

Several species of terebinth are common in the Holy Land and they are referred to in the Scriptures in different contexts.

A variety of the small mastic-shrub (*P. lentiscus*) yields resin, perhaps the 'balm' that Jacob's sons took as a gift to their brother in Egypt, while the two terebinth trees, which also yield resin, have the small edible nut which they took as well (Genesis 43:11, see Liquidambar pp. 48-49). The large Atlantic terebinths are often confused with oak trees which have a similar appearance; thus, the 'great oak' tree in which Absalom was hung by his hair was probably a terebinth – 2 Samuel 18:9. (The pistachio nut tree is often considered to be a biblical plant but it originates in Central Asia and was introduced to the Holy Land much later.)

Cultivation

They all need greenhouse protection (10-12°C) in cooler climates, or in milder areas plant against a wall.

Propagation is by cuttings in a frame in late summer.

Species

Pistacia atlantica, Atlantic terebinth, S.W. Asia and N. Africa

P. lentiscus, mastic, lentisc, Mediterranean region, about 1m (3ft)

P. terebinthus (*P. palaestina*) Palestine terebinth, turpentine tree, Mediterranean region, 3-5m (9-15ft) (see pl. 109)

Castor-oil Plant (*Ricinus*)

Following the Greek Septuagint version of the Old Testament, the castor-oil plant is said to be the plant that shaded Jonah while he waited to see what would become of the wicked city of Nineveh (Jonah 4:6-7); other versions call it a 'gourd'. The castor-oil plant certainly grows quickly in warm, rich soil, such as rubbish tips outside cities in hot countries. It is a man-size shrub with large, palmately lobed leaves. The flower spikes have separate male and female flowers: the bristly round fruits contain the poisonous mottled seeds that yield castor oil, used medicinally and as a lubricant.

Cultivation

Although a shrub in hot countries, it can be grown as a tall bedding plant in temperate areas. Seeds soaked for twenty-four hours and sown in individual pots with bottom heat should be planted out when danger of frost is past.

Species

Ricinus communis, castor bean, castor-oil plant or tree, palma christi, tropics and sub-tropics (see pl. 110). There is a decorative purple-leaved variety

Pl. 110. Castor-oil plant *Ricinus communis*.

Sandarac Tree, Thyine, or Citron Wood (*Tetraclinis*)

Right at the end of the Bible, in Revelation 18:12, several plant products imported into Rome are listed, including thyine or citron wood. It is a fragrant, reddish, ornamental timber used for veneers and fine quality cabinets in classical times. The tree is known as sandarac (*Tetraclinis articulata*) in North Africa and it is like a slender cypress, but with four-valved cones. The sandarac resin exudes from the trunk and is used for varnishes.

Pl. 110a. Sandarac tree *Tetraclinis articulata*.

Cultivation

This tree is too tender to survive in England or anywhere where frosts occur, but it will thrive in a cool greenhouse. Plants can be raised from cuttings or seeds and grown on in light soil. Isolated trees are like cypresses, but I have seen them in Cyprus grown as a clipped hedge.

Species

Tetraclinis articulata (*Callitris articulata*) sandarac tree, thyine or citron wood, Algeria, Morocco, Malta, evergreen conifer up to 15m (50ft) high (see pl. 110a)

Pl. 111. Christ thorn *Ziziphus spina-christi*.

Pl. 112. Crown of thorns, such as might have been used on Jesus.

Christ Thorn, Crown-of-Thorns (*Paliurus, Sarcopoterium, Ziziphus*)

In mockery the Roman soldiers crowned Jesus with thorns (Matthew 27:29; John 19:2) (see pls 111 and 112). We cannot be sure which plants were used but there are several candidates: the spiny burnet (*Sarcopoterium*), a low shrub common on the hills of the Holy Land; *Paliurus*, a shrub not now found in the Jerusalem area but further north; and *Ziziphus*, a small tree of the Dead Sea Valley. The latter two are both known as 'Christ thorn'. All of them have vicious thorns or prickles.

Cultivation

Seeds or plants may be difficult to obtain and they are tender, except *Paliurus*, which may be grown outside in temperate countries. The others are suitable for warm countries or greenhouse cultivation.

Species

Paliurus spina-christi, Christ thorn, S. Europe, 2-3m (6-10ft), small yellow/green flowers, flat winged fruits (see fig. 69)

Sarcopoterium spinosum (*Poterium spinosum*), spiny burnet, Mediterranean region, undershrub 15-30cm (6-12in.) high, greenish flowers in short spikes, round red fruit

Ziziphus spina-christi, Christ thorn, S.W. Asia and N. Africa, shrub or small tree, small flowers, yellow olive-like fruit sweet and juicy with 1-3 hard seeds which germinate easily at high temperatures (see fig. 69 and pls 111 and 112). *Z. lotus* is similar

Fig. 69. Christ thorns: A-C *Paliurus spina-christi*, D-F *Ziziphus spina-christi*.

How to Use the Plants you Grow

In the notes under each species, I sometimes mention a use to which you can put the plants. Having grown them, why not use them? You can probably think of other uses, but if you are unfamiliar with some of the species, you may find the following lists a helpful guide. Some species can be placed in several categories, and these groupings may provide ideas for the planning of your Bible garden, too.

Herbs and spices
Dill (p. 14), black mustard (p. 15), coriander and cumin (p. 17), black cumin (p. 22), horseradish (p. 32), saffron (p. 33), fennel (p. 34), mint (p. 37), marjoram (p. 38), rue (p. 40), sage (p. 41), bay (p. 48), myrtle (p. 53), rock-rose (p. 45), aloe (p. 79), frankincense (p. 80), capers (p. 81), cinnamon and cassia (p. 83), myrrh (p. 84), nard (p. 85), henna (p. 86)

Fruits and nuts
Fig (p. 46), walnut (p. 64), mulberry (p. 52), olive (p. 54), apricot and apple (p. 50), almond (p. 55), pomegranate (p. 56), grapevine (p. 59), date palm (p. 87), pistachio (p. 88)

Vegetables and cereals
Leek, onion, garlic (p. 14), cucumber and melon (p. 18), barley (p. 19), sorghum (p. 25), wheat (p. 26), chicory, lettuce, eryngo, sow-thistle (p. 32), vine leaves (p. 59), mustard seedlings (p. 15)

Fibres, textiles and baskets
Flax (p. 20), cotton (p. 86), willow, poplar (p. 69), papyrus (p. 73), reeds (p. 75), reed-mace, bulrush (p. 76), date-palm (p. 87)

Cut flowers, dried flower displays and greenery
Crown daisy (p. 16), barley (p. 19), flax (p. 20), mallows (p. 35), poppy (p. 23), thistles (p. 24), sorghum (p. 25), wheat (p. 26), anemone (p. 30), eryngo (p. 32), lily (p. 35), narcissus (p. 37), star-of-Bethlehem (p. 39), tulip (p. 42), box (p. 44), Judas tree (p. 45), rock-rose (p. 45), bay tree (p. 48), storax (p. 48), myrtle (p. 53), pomegranate (p 56), broom (p. 57), rose (p. 58). tamarisk (p. 59), cedar (p. 62), cypress (p. 63), juniper (p. 65), pine (p. 66), oak (p. 70), poplar and willow (p. 69), papyrus (p. 73), water-lily (p. 74), reeds (p. 75), reed-mace (p. 76), rushes (p. 76), oleander (p. 87), date palm (p. 87), castor bean (p. 81), sandarac (p.89), thorns (p. 90)

Pot-pourri
Crown daisy (p. 16), poppy (p. 23), wormwood (p. 31), fennel (p. 34), mint (p. 37), marjoram (p. 38), rue (p. 40), sage (p. 41), box (p. 44), rock-rose (p. 41), bay (p. 48), myrtle (p. 53), pomegranate (p. 56), rose (p.58), juniper (p. 65), sweet cane (p. 72), water-lily (p. 74), nard (p. 85), henna (p. 86), terebinth (p. 88)

Conservation of wildlife
Insects such as butterflies, hover-flies and bees enjoy many of these flowers; seed-eating birds like thistles, etc. A pool extends the diversity of wildlife, especially if designed with that in mind.

Medicinal
Dill (p. 14), coriander (p. 17, cumin seeds (p.17), mallow (p. 35), rue (p. 40), rock-rose (p. 45), olives (p. 54), aloe (p. 79), castor-oil plant (p. 81)

Cereals in the author's own Bible garden.

Bibliography

Some general gardening books

Bailey, H.B. & E.Z. (eds.) *Hortus Third*. A concise dictionary of plants cultivated in the USA and Canada. New York: Macmillan Publishing Company. 1976

Bean, W.J., *Trees and Shrubs Hardy in the British Isles*. 8th revised ed. by D.L. Clarke. London: John Murray 4 vols. 1970-80

Everett, Tom H. (ed.), *New York Botanical Garden Illustrated Encyclopedia of Horticulture*. New York: Garland Publishers 1980 on, 10 vols.

Graf, A.B. *Tropica* Second edition 1981. New Jersey: Roehrs

Grey-Wilson, Christopher & Mathew, Brian, *Bulbs: the Bulbous Plants of Europe and their Allies*. London: Collins 1981

Griffiths, Mark (ed.), *Index of Garden Plants*. London: Macmillan 1994

Hillier's Manual of Trees and Shrubs. Newton Abbot: David & Charles 5th ed. 1981

Huxley, Anthony and Mark Griffiths (eds.), *The New Royal Horticultural Dictionary of Gardening*. London: Macmillan 1992 4 vols.

Jellito, L. & Schacht, W. *Hardy herbaceous perennials*. Third edition Schacht, W. & Fessler, A. Portland, Oregon: Timber Press

Mathew, Brian, *Dwarf Bulbs*. London: Batsford & RHS 1973

Pearson, Robert (ed.), *The Wisley Book of Gardening*. London: Collingridge & Royal Horticultural Society 1981

Reader's Digest Illustrated Guide to Gardening. London: Reader's Digest Association 1975

Rothchild, M. & Farrell, C., *The Butterfly Gardener*. London: Rainbird Press 1983

Titchmarsh, Alan, *Creating Garden Pools*. London: Hamlyn 1986

Turner, A. & Baker, H., *Grapes Indoors and Out*. Wisley Handbook. London: Royal Horticultural Society

Some books on Bible plants and nature

Alon, Azaria, *The Natural History of the Land of the Bible*. New York: Doubleday & Co. Inc. 1978

Greenoak, Francesca. *God's Acre. The Flowers and Animals of the Parish Churchyard*. London: Orbis 1985

Hareuveni, Nogah, *Ecology in the Bible* (1974). *Nature in our Biblical Heritage* (1980). *Tree and Shrub in our Biblical Heritage* (1984). *Desert and Shepherd in our Biblical Heritage* (1991). Israel: Neot Kedumim, Kiryat Ono

Hepper, F. Nigel, *Bible Plants at Kew*. London: HMSO 1981, reprinted 1985

Hepper, F. Nigel, *Illustrated Encyclopedia of Bible Plants*. Leicester: Inter-Varsity Press/Grand Rapids: Baker Book House 1992

Hillier, N., Johnson, J.D. & Wiseman, D.J. (eds.) *The Illustrated Bible Dictionary*. Leicester: Inter-Varsity Press 3 vols. 1980. Botanical entries by F. Nigel Hepper.

James, Wilma, *Gardening with Biblical Plants*. Chicago: Nelson-Hall 1983

King, Eleanor Anthony, *Bible Plants for American Gardens*. New York: Macmillan 1941; Dover edition 1975

MacKay, Alastair I., *Farming and Gardening in the Bible*. Emmaus, Penn: Rodale Press 1950

Moldenke, H.N. & A.L., *Plants of the Bible*. New York: Ronald Press Co. 1952

Plitmann, U., Heyn, C., Danin, A., & Shmida, A., *Pictorial Flora of Israel*. Jerusalem: Massada Ltd. 1983. (Hebrew text, English preface and index, 750 colour photos of plants with scientific names and distribution maps)

Swenson, Allan A., *Your Biblical Garden*. New York: Doubleday & Co. Inc. 1981

Zohary, Michael, *Plants of the Bible*. Cambridge University Press 1982

Zohary, M. & Feinbrun-Dothan, N., *Flora Palaestina*. Jerusalem: Israel Academy of Science 8 vols. 1966-86

PLANT SOURCES

Canada

The Canadian Plant Source Book. Anne & Peter Ashley, 93 Fentiman Avenue, Ottawa, ON KIS OT7. 16,000 hardy plants available at retail and wholesale nurseries across Canada, including those who ship to U.S.A. English common names and English and French cross-indexes.

Germany

Pflanzen-Einkaufsführer. (1995) Anne & Walter Erhardt. Verlag Eugen Ulmer, PO Box 70 05 61, D-70574 Stuttgart. ISBN 3-8001-6544-9. Some 60,000 plants from 460 European nurseries.

Great Britain

The Fruit and Veg Finder. HDRA, Ryton-on-Dunmore, Coventry CV8 3LG. Produced in association with Brogdale Horticultural Trust. The 5th edition lists sources and descriptions for more than 3,000 vegetable varieties and almost 1,300 fruits, from a total of about 200 suppliers. ISBN 0-905343-20-4.

The RHS Plant Finder. Tony Lord (ed.) Annually updated listing of plant species and nurseries. ISBN 0-9512161-8-X. Royal Horticultural Society, Vincent Square, London SW1P 2PE

Netherlands

Plantenvinder voor de Lage Landen. (1995/96). ed. Sarah Hart. Terra, Uitgeverij TERRA, Postbus 188, 7200AD Zutphen. ISBN 90-6255-623-X. Approx 40,000 plants and 110 nurseries.

USA

The Andersen's Horticultural Library's Source List of Plants and Seeds. Andersen Horticultural Library, Minnesota Landscape Arboretum, 3675 Arboretum Drive, Box 39, Chanhassen, MN 55317. Compiled by Richard Isaacson. (4th ed. 1996). All are prepared to ship interstate.

Cornucopia – A Source Book of Edible Plants. (1990). Stephen Facciola, Kampong Publications, 1870 Sunrise Drive, Vista, California 92084. A very substantial and comprehensive volume (678pp.) which documents 3,000 species of edible plants and 7,000 cultivars available in the USA and abroad. A software version for Microsoft Windows is available. ISBN 0-9628087-0-9.

Gardening by Mail. (1994). 4th ed. Barbara J. Barton. Houghton Mifflin Co., 222 Berkeley Street, Boston, MA 02114, USA. A directory of mail order resources for gardeners in the USA and Canada, including seed companies, nurseries, suppliers of all garden necessaries and ornaments, horticultural and plant societies, magazines, libraries and books.

Perennials: A Nursery Source Manual. (1989). ed. Barbara Pesch. Brooklyn Botanic Garden, 1000 Washington Avenue, Brooklyn, NY 11225-1099. ISBN 0-945352-48-4. Lists 320 nurseries and some 4000 perennials.

Taylor's Guide to Speciality Nurseries. (1993). Barbara R. Barton ed. Houghton Mifflin Co. 222 Berkeley Street, Boston, MA 02114, USA. Over 300 nurseries in the USA selling ornamental garden plants, all of which will ship.

Useful Information

Some Bible gardens in various parts of the world

Australia
Bible Garden, 12 Mitchell Road, Palm Beach, NSW – founded in 1962 by Gerald H. Robinson and maintained by the Memorial Trust; descriptive booklet available

St Paul's Cathedral, Sydney NSW 2000 – proposed by Jane Cleary 1994

Rockhampton Botanic Garden, Queensland – a biblical garden with terraces, waterfall, desert and oasis, designed 1986 for the City Council

Canada
Alberta – proposal by Don MacKenzie, Black Diamond, Alberta TOL OHO, 1994

England
Bolton Churches Bible Garden, Lancs. – Revd Richard Hambly co-ordinator

Holy Trinity Parish Church, Sheen Park, Richmond, Surrey – 1994 planting of small garden around car park

Millennium Bible Garden, Woodbridge, Suffolk – Nicholas Green co-ordinator

Royal Botanic Gardens, Kew, Richmond, Surrey – separate Bible garden, proposed 1997, also many biblical plants may be seen growing outside or in the greenhouses, and plant products are kept in the Museum; see *Bible Plants at Kew* by F. Nigel Hepper (currently out of print)

St James's Church, Piccadilly, London – God's Garden including biblical species, started 1986 – currently in abeyance

St Mark's, Isle of Man, – Millennium Bible Garden – Bob Easton designer

St Michael's Convent, Ham Common, Richmond, Surrey

Sternberg Centre for Judaism, The Manor House, 80 East End Road, London N3 2SY – active 1997

Ireland
St Benedict's Priory, The Mount, Cobh, Co. Cork – completed 1994-5

Israel
Neot Kedumim (Biblical Landscape Reserve in Israel), Kiryat Ono, between Tel Aviv and Jerusalem – founded in the 1970s by Nogah Hareuveni, 550 acres of hillside with biblical and traditional Jewish plants in a natural setting; see the guidebook, *Ecology in the Bible* and other books in the Bibliography

St George's College (beside St George's Cathedral), PO Box 1248, Jerusalem, planned by F. Nigel Hepper 1990, active 1997

Italy
Ara Viridis Project, Franciscan Center of Environmental Studies, Via del Serafico, 1,00142 Rome – projected 1989

Netherlands
Amsterdam Free University, van de Boechortstraat 8, Amsterdam – a Bible garden is being planned (1987) by Daan Smit, Curator of the University Hortus Botanicus, who organised the massive exhibition, 'Plants of the Bible', to celebrate the University's centenary in 1980

New Zealand
Rutland Street Chapel, Christchurch – designed by Dr David Given, 1986 – active 1997

Scotland
Eredine Christian Trust, Argyll Tel. 01866 844207

Elgin Cathedral – 1995 onwards – managed by Donald McBean, Chief Horticultural Officer

South Africa
Johannesburg Botanical Garden – 'Bible plant' section is planned

Spain
Projectista de Jardineria y Paisaje, Torquemada, 28043 Madrid – proposed for Toledo 1990

USA
Messiah Lutheran Church, 5740 W. Holt Road, Holt, MI 48842 – active 1996

Temple Beth-El (Synagogue), 70 Orchard Avenue, Providence 6, Rhode Island – active 1996

Cathedral Church of St John the Divine, 1047 Amsterdam Avenue, New York – garden founded in 1973 by the late Mrs Sarah Larkin Loening in the grounds of the church; open sunrise to sunset; guide booklet available

Magnolia Plantation and Gardens, Route 4, Charleston, South Carolina 29407 – Bible garden founded in 1983 by J. Drayton Hastie as part of the Gardens; open to the public; guide booklet available

Missouri Botanical Garden, St Louis, Missouri – many of the biblical species are grown in the Shoenberg Temperate House and special exhibits are staged from time to time; descriptive leaflet available

San Francisco – Strybing Arboretum, Golden Gate Park – Jewish; booklet issued

St James' Lutheran Church, 110 Avenue Phoenetia, Coral Gables, Florida – the Garden of Our Lord; open to the public

Warsaw Biblical Gardens, PO Box 1223, Warsaw IN 46580 – designed 1987; not known whether constructed

Wales
Bangor Cathedral Close, Bangor, Caernarvon – garden founded in 1962 by Dr Tatham Whitehead and maintained by Arfon Borough Council, Caernarvon; open at all times; guide booklet (out of print)

Some useful addresses

Australia
Royal Horticultural Society of
New South Wales
GPOB 4728, Sydney NSW 2001

Great Britain
Amateur Entomologist's Society
355 Hounslow Road, Hanworth, Middx. TW13 SJH; for literature on butterfly plants etc.

Herb Society
77 Great Peter Street, London SWlP 2EZ; the Society's journal *The Herbal Review* lists herb farms and suppliers

MBF (Clansman) Ltd.,
144 Neilston Road, Paisley PA2 6QJ; for labels, marking pens etc.

National Association of Flower Arranging Societies of Great Britain
21a Denbigh Street, London SW1

Royal Horticultural Society
Vincent Square, London SWlP 2PE; for the journal *The Garden* and *RHS Plantfinder* listing suppliers

Royal Society for the Protection of Birds
Sandy, Beds.; for publications on garden birds

Veritas Nursery (Craig Jamieson) – specialises in biblical plants and seeds: Tel. 01465 713388

Israel
Society for the Protection of Nature (SPNI)
4 Hashfela St., Tel Aviv 66183

Neot Kedumim (Biblical Landscape Reserve in Israel) Kiryat Ono, PO Box 299

Tantur Biblical Resources Study Center
near Bethlehem

South Africa
Pretoria Horticultural Society
POB 1186, Pretoria 0001

USA
American Horticultural Society
Mount Vernon Va 22121; publishers of *American Horticulturist,* with names of suppliers

California Horticultural Society
c/o California Academy of Sciences, San Francisco CA 94118; publishers of *Pacific Horticulture,* which names suppliers

Index of References in the Bible

Note: the references provided in the text are very selective but they provide at least one reference to each plant or plant product mentioned in chapters 1-6.

Index of Plant Names

Common English and the scientific names are indexed alphabetically.
The plant family to which each species belongs is enclosed in round brackets.

Page references are given in roman.

Black-and-white figures are in *italic numbers*.

Plate numbers are in **bold** for the photographs.